The *Mindfulness* Budget

The *Mindfulness* Budget

Using Mindful Techniques to Improve
Your Financial Health

Madonna Gauding

Leaping Hare Press

First published in the UK in 2010 by

Leaping Hare Press

210 High Street, Lewes
East Sussex BN7 2NS, UK
www.leapingharepress.co.uk

Text copyright © Madonna Gauding 2010
Design and layout copyright © Ivy Press Limited 2010

British Library Cataloguing-in-Publication Data
A catalogue record for this book is available from
the British Library

ISBN: 978-1-907332-41-8

This book was conceived, designed and produced by

Leaping Hare Press

Creative Director PETER BRIDGEWATER
Publisher JASON HOOK
Art Director WAYNE BLADES
Senior Editor POLITA ANDERSON
Designer BERNARD HIGTON
Illustrator SARAH YOUNG

Printed in China
Colour Origination by Ivy Press Reprographics

10 9 8 7 6 5 4 3 2 1

CONTENTS

MONEY & MINDFULNESS

Mindfulness helps you bring consciousness to your relationship with money: why you struggle with it, what you think and how you feel about it, and how you can make peace with it. Simply paying attention can help you relax the grip money has on your life and set financial priorities that reflect your deepest needs and highest values.

WHAT IS MONEY?

◆

*Money is a wonderful invention that symbolises our interconnected-
ness and our need for one another. It allows us to be compensated for
something we do well and to pay others to do things we cannot or
choose not to do for ourselves — such as grow our food, build our houses
or make our clothes. Money frees us from the restriction of the early
barter system, where we had to deal directly with the individuals
who provided our goods and services. If no one was around to help us
raise our barn, forge our tools or cut our hair, we were out of luck.*

WITH THE INVENTION of money came the freedom to
buy goods and services, at any time, from anyone,
anywhere. Money opens up endless creative possibilities, and
the opportunity to live in comfort, accrue wealth and create
happiness for ourselves and others.

Without money there would be no civilisation or the
leisure time to grow intellectually and spiritually. Without
money, we would each be stuck in an isolated brutish struggle
to survive. Unfortunately, in many parts of the world,
survival is still an issue, and poverty is a way of life. A more
equitable access to money and resources is the answer to
lacking materials or possessions, along with local economic
development that serves the people. For example, simple
micro-lending programmes have lifted women out of poverty
in India and other third-world countries.

What Money Can Buy

Because of money many of us live in comfort beyond what medieval royalty could have imagined. We have central heating in our homes and air-conditioning in our cars, plus plentiful food from all over the world. We have communication systems and methods of transportation beyond anything a medieval prince could have imagined. Our health care extends our lives, and the Internet gives us unimaginable knowledge at our fingertips. And unlike the kings and queens of old, we have entertainment available around the clock. If you are feeling poor, just imagine how astonished your ancestors would be at what you own, and how comfortably you live.

A Double-edged Sword

Money is a brilliant invention of the human mind, a tool that can be used for individual and social good. But money can feel like a double-edged sword. Even though it has given us incomparable wealth compared to past eras, it probably causes more suffering, pain and confusion than ever before. We have trouble earning it, managing it and making wise decisions when it comes to spending it.

It is often said that 'money is the root of all evil'. But our problems are not rooted in money, but in our human nature. Buddhists would say that we suffer because we feel a 'continuous lack' for something without which we feel incomplete. If only we had a richer spouse, a bigger home, a holiday home,

a better job, a holiday at the beach, a new car, a bigger income, a bigger savings account, a flat-screen TV, or perhaps a beef-burger or pizza at this moment, we would feel satisfied and whole. Money seems to be essential for making most of our desires come true. It can be a vehicle for happiness, but our desires keep us perennially dissatisfied.

'No Man is an Island'

Our misconception that things are solid and permanent also contributes to our chronic disappointment. The new car becomes dented, the new shoes become dated and the new kitchen gadget we 'had to have' sits idle on the worktop. Life is change and there is nothing and no one permanent to cling to. To add insult to injury, we discover that we are not the solid, separate, independent person we imagine ourselves to be. We imagine we are captain of our own ship and we rise and fall dependent on our own talents and actions, but the truth is something else. We are profoundly interdependent with, and dependent on, others and all of existence. The Buddha taught this 2,500 years ago, and physicists confirm his teachings today.

The Path to Mindfulness

The Buddha taught that money does not make us whole and complete – nor will anything or anyone else. This is his first Noble Truth – that the nature of life is suffering. His second Noble Truth is that suffering comes from *desiring* and being *attached* to things, money, people or experiences, but not from *enjoying* them. The third is that we can stop our suffering around money and anything else, and the fourth is that there is a way to do that, a path that we can follow. Mindfulness is one aspect of the eight-fold path of the Buddha that we will concentrate on in this book. Mindfulness offers a powerful way to remove suffering from our relationship with money. By creating a Mindfulness Budget, a way of managing finances based on the practice of mindfulness, we can shift from desiring and attachment to pleasure and enjoyment.

WHEN IT COMES TO MONEY,
WE ARE ALL IRRATIONAL

We may say we want to save for retirement, buy fewer clothes, eat out less or give up our addiction to buying antiques — and we mean it — but, somehow, we never manage to do so. For centuries classical economists assumed that when it comes to money, we make logical, rational, self-interested decisions in which we always weigh costs against benefits, and choose the best value and the highest profit for ourselves. Supposedly, we are all intelligent, analytical beings who have perfect self-discipline in pursuit of our future goals. Unfortunately these abstract, tidy economic theories have nothing to do with how we actually behave, think or feel.

WHEN WE EXAMINE our financial lives, we usually find all sorts of irrational, self-sabotaging behaviour, random acts of selfless generosity, and the occasional balanced current account. Clearly, when it comes to money we are complex, psychological, unpredictable and vulnerable. As the Buddha saw so clearly, we may have the best intentions and think we are perfectly rational, but we are often ruled by our desires and emotions, which cause us much suffering in every area of our lives.

About 20 years ago, a new discipline emerged called 'behavioural economics'. It applies psychology to the study of how people make economic choices, and directly challenges outdated and unrealistic economic theories. Behavioural economists focused on the fundamental tension, in humans and other animals, between seizing available rewards in the present, and being patient for better rewards in the future. We all want instant gratification, and to get better rewards in the future.

Making Choices

If we are asked the question, 'Which do you want right now, a fruit basket or a pizza?', you may say, 'Pizza!' if you love pizza. But if asked, 'Which one do you want a week from now?', you may say, 'The fruit basket.' It is easy to put off the better, more healthy choice for the future, but harder to choose it in the present moment.

We struggle in life because we choose the wrong things, or spend too much on what we want now at the expense of those things we might want and need in the future. We buy on credit something we may not need and can't afford, and because of the additional interest we pay, we have less money to buy those things we really need now and want in the future.

Present & Future

According to classical economic theory, there shouldn't be any disconnect between what we are doing now and what we want to be doing in the future, nor between our values and how we live now, but we are all intimately familiar with that disconnect. We may feel distressed and confused by our overspending,

our impulsive buying, our debt or our financial disorganis-
ation, but we can take heart that we are not alone. These
tendencies are a result of our human nature where we are torn
between wanting things right now and thoughtfully planning
for the future. There is no need to have shame or guilt. But
there are things we can do to end our financial suffering and
help ourselves achieve what we really do want. We can start
with being mindful of our basic human nature, which will
allow us to find creative ways to override the emotions and
desires that can harm us financially and in other ways.

The Ancient Greek's View on Instant Gratification

The ancient Greek poet Homer gave us the Odyssey, *the great story of the hero Odysseus and his journey to return home after the Trojan War. In this story Homer has Odysseus confront his desire for instant gratification, which is in conflict with what he really wants — to return to his beloved Ithaca and his wife Penelope.*

I N THE STORY, the goddess Circe informs Odysseus that his ship will pass the island of the Sirens, whose irresistible singing can lure sailors to steer towards them and on to rocks. The Sirens of course are a wonderful metaphor for our desires and appetites, the power of their seductions and the pitfalls they represent. In today's world our Sirens may be a large flat-screen TV, a date at a five-star restaurant or an expensive wardrobe bought on sale — none of which we can afford but we imagine will make us happy. Any of our Sirens could lead us to crash on the rocky shores of credit card debt.

Resisting Temptation

In Homer's story Circe advises Odysseus to prepare for the temptations to come, and tells him to order his crew to fill their ears with wax so they cannot hear the Sirens' songs. But *he* may hear the Sirens' beautiful voices without risk if he commands his sailors to tie him to the ship's mast and ignore

his pleas for release until they have passed beyond danger. In this way Odysseus commits to what he wants in the future according to the values he holds dear. By binding himself to the mast he prevents his desire for instant gratification from undermining what he really wants – to get home to his wife Penelope and his rightful place as king of Ithaca. Yet he is still free to enjoy the song of the Sirens. In other words, life does not have to be miserable if we rein in our desires and emotions in the present moment when they undermine what we really want. As Odysseus demonstrated, you can still have pleasure and enjoy life even if you forego the large flat-screen TV.

Commitment to Our Values

Through the practice of mindfulness, we can become aware of our personal emotional triggers, our unhelpful ideas about money and the seductions of advertising. When we acknowledge our unhelpful patterns and behaviours, it will soon become clear to us that they conflict with our higher values. Then, we can learn to identify with and commit to our higher values and other strategies, to override our faulty thinking and get around our desire for instant gratification. We also can commit to our real values to counteract our tendency to procrastinate on matters that require immediate effort for a future pay-off – like keeping track of our expenses, putting money away in a savings bank or learning a new skill that will help us get a better job.

THE ROLE OF EMOTION &
DESIRE IN FINANCIAL DECISIONS

When making choices in the marketplace we may think we are objectively comparing one car, or refrigerator, or suit to another; but our choice really depends on how we describe the objects in relation to ourselves. We may say 'this suit is sexy and sophisticated', or 'that car will make me feel powerful'. Furthermore we are vulnerable to how things are advertised, as advertising frames the potential purchase in a way that uses emotional and cultural cues to influence our decision. A car is sold not as a vehicle for transportation, but as a symbol of affluence, youth or sexual attractiveness. A chocolate bar is sold as a blissful, sensual, ecstatic eating experience.

WE RARELY BUY SOMETHING in a vacuum, but rather we make our decisions in the context of other similar items. For example, we usually compare shop prices to decide which TV, car or refrigerator we want. An appliance shop may offer three models of a washing machine: low, medium, and high priced. The items are priced and presented so that you will buy the middle priced one, which is the one the shop really wants to sell. The high priced item is there to make the middle priced one appear to be a better deal. Advertising is very powerful. How often do advertisers succeed in selling us something we don't even need, or get us to buy it at a higher price than it's worth? We may think of ourselves as very

intelligent, savvy consumers, yet how many things do we own that we regret having bought? How many mistakes hang in the back of our wardrobes unworn and forgotten?

The Best Things in Life…

We may nod our heads knowingly when someone says 'Money can't buy happiness' or 'The best things in life are free', but our behaviour says otherwise. When we are depressed, or lonely, or feel unloved, we often buy something to make us feel better. Perhaps a new outfit, a new car, a trip to the Bahamas, a tub of ice cream, a drink at a bar or a new pet. When we want to celebrate we buy a bottle of champagne, a dinner out or a chocolate cake. It is the same if we are bored. We buy something to make us feel better. In the modern age, because of advertising and the consumer culture in which we live, we are wired to satisfy our psychological, emotional and spiritual needs with physical consumption. Again, this is nothing to feel ashamed about. This is how we are today and what we have to work with.

That said, our irrationalities and emotional triggers are a part of us as human beings and have been so since we first walked the earth. These are the desires and emotions the Buddha identified that can lead us to suffering. Through the practice of mindfulness we can get to know our desires and our emotional and financial triggers and vulnerabilities and develop strategies to prevent them getting the better of us.

WHAT YOU WILL LEARN
IN THIS BOOK

◆

In Part I you will learn about mindfulness, a meditative practice that has its origins in the teachings of Shakyamuni Buddha, the founder of Buddhism. Although it is an ancient practice, it is also a timeless one, and well suited for our modern lifestyle. If anything, because of the complexity of modern life, the practice of mindfulness is needed more today than when the Buddha introduced it over several thousand years ago. Everyday stress causes many of us to pull into our shell and live life as if on automatic pilot.We numb ourselves with unhealthy habits and various addictions just to get through the day.

SOMETIMES SHOPPING and overspending is our response to money problems. Unfortunately, credit cards allow us to ignore reality and pretend, for the moment, that we have no debt. If this sounds familiar to you, then mindfulness practice can help you breathe, slow down and reconnect in the present moment with what is going on with yourself and the world around you. From this alive and aware place, firmly rooted in reality, you can begin to make better decisions in all areas of your life – including how you manage your money. And you don't need to be a Buddhist to practise mindfulness. Today mindfulness is taught in many hospital settings – for pain management, for stress reduction and for help in healing from serious diseases. These practices are the basis for living a

more conscious and aware life, as well as for transforming your relationship with money. As you will discover, mindfulness, combined with self-love and compassion, can set you free.

Your Relationship With Money

In Part II you will examine your past and present relationship to money. You will explore what you learnt about money from your family and others. Because you may have beliefs about money that are holding you back, closely examining those beliefs will help you decide whether or not they are serving you well. You are not alone if you have financial fears – fear about not having enough money to retire, fear about losing your money in the stock market or fear of losing your job. Getting these fears out in the open, and exploring ways to mitigate them, will help you heal your relationship to money.

You may also have unrealistic fantasies about money – that you will win the lottery, or meet a wealthy man or woman who will take care of you for the rest of your life, or that with the right advice on the stock market you will make a fortune. You may daydream about living in luxury in a mansion overlooking the ocean. Fantasies are fun but they can be a way to avoid dealing with your actual financial situation.

Letting go of your financial past and addressing your money secrets will help you to move forwards…

Keeping Secrets

Many of us are more reticent about disclosing the details of our financial lives than we are about our sex lives. You may have shame, guilt and regret about your past financial mistakes and money secrets you do not want anyone to know. Letting go of your financial past and addressing your money secrets will help you to move forwards into a healthier guilt-, shame- and regret-free future. You will explore how your views about yourself and money may make you vulnerable to advertising, and how you can use mindfulness to gain control over your spending. If you don't earn enough money, you may need to examine why that is so and what is holding you back.

Exploring Your Values

Most of us have a set of values we try to live by. Exploring your values and how they influence your financial life can shed light on why you may have financial problems. You may have a 'disconnect' between your values and your relationship with money that, if brought into harmony, could transform your life. Wealth is often understood to mean how much money one has, yet it can mean so much more. Expanding your definition of wealth and practising gratitude can ease your financial fears and help bring your financial life into perspective. Your financial life not only affects you but also the earth and everyone and everything on it. What we choose to consume makes a difference to the health of the environment and affects the lives of others.

Mindfulness is the practice of becoming aware of what you ordinarily ignore or simply haven't been able to feel or understand. Paying close attention to your feelings, thoughts and the world around you opens up your life in ways you may have yet to experience. Using mindfulness to pay close attention to how you relate to money and using what you learn to make positive changes is the core of this book.

Back to Basics

In Part III you will begin to focus on Mindfulness Budget Basics, starting with a statement of your financial goals for the next year, and then extending to five years, ten years and 25 years. You will then calculate your income, your expenses and your debt. And from there you will look at each major area of your budget such as housing, food, clothing and entertainment, but with a bit of a twist. Using mindfulness you will look at how your beliefs, thoughts and emotions affect your expenditure and what you can do in each area of spending to help yourself stay on track, live by your values and reach your financial goals. Like Odysseus, you will learn how to avoid the rocky shores of financial distress, have more joy and pleasure in life, and ultimately reach where you want to go.

RECORDING YOUR INSIGHTS

To make the most progress with the Mindfulness Budget it will help you to keep a Mindfulness Budget journal, either handwritten or on your computer. Use whichever method works best for you. You will be asked to use your journal for the following reasons:

• **To keep a record of what you spend.** Starting now, record what you spend every day, no matter how small the amount. Recording what you spend is a mindfulness practice that helps you to become conscious of what you are spending and how it is affecting your life.

• **To record your insights when doing an exercise.** Many of the exercises throughout the book ask you to write as part of the exercise. Writing helps you to stay in the present and bring to consciousness thoughts and feelings that you may not have been aware of.

• **To express your thoughts and feelings about your relationship to money.** Write a poem, draw a picture, compose a song or simply jot down insights as they occur. Feel free to write about your struggles and your discoveries, and to express your emotions. This will help you in your journey towards a healthy financial life.

• **To identify which expenses are absolutely necessary.**
Whilst some expenses are necessary, others might be undermining your financial goals. Try to be as accurate as possible
about the amounts you are spending.

• **To help maintain a loving attitude towards yourself.**
Use your journal to remind yourself that it is difficult not only
for you, but for others to negotiate in today's financial world.
Be sure to express compassion for yourself and others.

• **To practise mindfulness.** The act of recording your
insights in your journal helps you stay mindful about how you
relate to money, how you use it in your life, and in what ways
it affects your body, mind and emotions.

• **To heal your relationship with money.** Writing in your
journal will help you process your past and current financial
difficulties, so you can begin to create a satisfying financial life.
By creating your Mindfulness Budget you can give yourself a
fresh start.

The traditional approach to financial advice assumes that we
have money problems because we are not living up to the
rational model of economics. In other words, we are not
clear-headed or rational enough in our approach. All we need,
it seems, is a good calculator, good record-keeping skills and

a good dose of self-discipline and willpower. Such advice ignores that we are *all* complex, emotional human beings who each struggle with money in our own way. Traditional advice leads us to believe we have problems with money because we are lacking in some way. We are 'losers' in a world defined by 'winners'.

Tricks & Traps

Such a limited and false view ignores that money is both an individual and societal problem. The competitive cultures we live in, which thrive on the idea of scarcity, are often cut-throat and unforgiving. Financial tricks and traps await us at every turn, and it is easy to be manipulated or taken advantage of – just reading a credit card agreement or a mortgage agreement can be daunting. It is especially difficult to stay afloat in times when the economy takes a turn for the worse.

Remember that this is a journey to find financial balance and sanity in a difficult world. This transition involves learning new information, having patience and practising loving kindness towards yourself, as you bring congruence to your values and your financial life. Whenever feelings of shame or guilt arise, simply acknowledge them and gently let them go. Do not allow them to be a constant companion in your thoughts. Congratulate yourself for having the courage to examine your life. There is no place in the Mindfulness Budget for self-reprimands and harsh judgements.

PART I

WHAT IS MINDFULNESS?

Mindfulness is present, engaged awareness.
It is a process of continual observation and attention as
you experience the ongoing flow of your changing sensory
awareness and perceptions. When you are mindful you are
not passive: you bring intention to whatever you are doing.
Mindfulness is paying attention, without judgement, to
what is going on inside of you, emotionally and
physically, and what is going on around you in your
environment. The practice of mindfulness applied to
your financial life will help you transform your
relationship with money.

THE PRESENT MOMENT
IS ALL YOU HAVE

◆

Mindfulness is a practice and an approach to life based on the understanding that the present is the only time any of us really have. Through attending to the present you can learn, perceive, change and heal. Through mindfulness you can access your own powerful inner resources for insight and transformation.

HOW DO YOU practise mindfulness? By choosing to pay attention, in the present moment, to your physical sensations, perceptions, emotions, thoughts and mental imagery. Mindfulness is the non-judgemental observation of what is going on with you right now, in this moment. You can also bring mindful awareness to any area of your life you may want to explore, such as your relationship to money. Because, like everyone, you have routines and habits, and they may prevent you from being fully aware of your moment-to-moment experience, or what you really think and feel. When you mindfully participate in life, you can replace your unconscious reactivity with a more accurate perception of what is going on, externally and internally. More accurate perception leads you to be a more effective actor in the world and to enjoy a greater sense of ease as you go about your daily life. When you develop moment-to-moment awareness, you gain a deeper, richer and more vital experience of living.

Contemporary Mindfulness

Mindfulness has its origins in the ancient practices of Buddhism and yoga but is now taught in contemporary form by Western teachers such as stress-reduction pioneer Jon Kabat-Zinn and Insight Meditation teachers Jack Kornfield and Sharon Salzberg. Contemporary culture enjoys extraordinary advances in science and technology and a level of physical comfort and wealth unknown in much of the world. Yet coupled with these advances is an increasing sense of pressure and sensory overload. People of all ages feel tremendous stress, which contributes to a variety of mental and physical problems. Mindful awareness invites you to stop, breathe, observe and connect with your inner experience. When you do, stress decreases.

Reasons to Be Mindful

In the last decade research has shown mindfulness to be effective in:

- Lowering blood pressure
- Boosting the immune system
- Increasing attention and focus
- Helping with anxiety and depression
- Fostering well-being
- Lessening emotional reactivity
- Thickening or strengthening the brain in areas related to decision making, emotional flexibility and empathy

Bringing mindful observation to areas of your life that may be troubling you, such as your relationship with money seems counter-intuitive. Your instinct may be to avoid putting a spotlight on what causes you stress. But through the mere act of mindful observation you can begin to unravel the physical, mental and emotional knots that hold you back from solving your financial problems with creativity and compassion.

YOUR NORMAL
STATE OF MIND

In your normal state of mind your thoughts usually jump from one to the other, each one triggering the next. For example, you may drive to work using your usual route, and be so lost in thought that you fail to notice anything along the way. In a state of mindfulness you may turn your attention to watching those thoughts as an impartial observer, or to noticing whether your body is feeling pain or cold or another sensation. You may become aware that the trees along your route are beginning to change, or that the lorry in front of you is driving a bit erratically, prompting more caution on your part.

THROUGH DELIBERATE FOCUSED AWARENESS you can take a break from being lost in your thoughts and in the emotions triggered by them, and turn your awareness to the present. Your senses will come alive, your sense of space will expand and

your experience of time will become more fluid. In the practice of mindfulness there is nothing but the present. Life lived fully in the present is, by nature, rich, full and deep.

With practice, mindfulness cultivates the possibility of freeing yourself of reactive, habitual patterns of thinking, feeling and acting, including impulsive spending or spending with no idea how much you have in your account. Mindfulness promotes balance by helping you avoid extremes of thought and action. It gives you the infinite opportunities and choices inherent in the present moment, whereas mentally living in the past or the future limits your possibilities. Mindfulness also promotes intelligence and wisdom because your mind is alive and fully awake, and mindfulness promotes compassion through non-judgemental acceptance of what is.

AN ANCIENT PRACTICE
FOR MODERN TIMES

The historical Buddha, Buddha Shakyamuni, lived in India around 500 BCE. He began life as a prince, and lived a sheltered, idyllic life where only young, beautiful people surrounded him. One day, out of curiosity, he left the palace compound and was shocked at the sight of old people, sick people and all manner of human suffering. He was so moved he left his privileged life and became a spiritual seeker. He wanted to discover how to remedy the pain he witnessed.

H E SET ABOUT WANDERING among like-minded people, trying various spiritual practices and engaging with the most respected teachers of the day. Ultimately, he became dissatisfied with the path he was following, and set out on his own to discover how to end suffering and understand the true meaning of life. After many years of trial and error he eventually achieved enlightenment. He did not plan to teach others how to do the same, but those close to him, seeing his transformation and his release from his own suffering, begged him to reveal his methods.

Living in the Present Moment

One of the most healing and effective practices the Buddha taught was the practice of mindfulness. He discovered that we create our world and our reality in the present moment, and therefore it is crucial to learn to pay attention to the present. He knew, by watching his own thoughts, that the human mind is constantly swinging into the future or back to the past, and spends very little time in the present. However, he was not saying that we should avoid memory or imagination and live in a strange eternal now. He did see that in order to get beyond our confusion and suffering we need to train ourselves to see how we distort reality by continually bringing the past and the future into the present. To cut our confusion he advocated that we practise being fully mindful of what is happening right now.

The Mind's Eye

Left to its own inclinations our mind would much rather construct a story about the present moment than see and experience it fresh and clear-eyed. For example, we may construct a believable story about why we should buy or even deserve the new expensive shoes we saw in a shop window, instead of seeing them for what they are – an attempt to take away the pain we feel today about being unappreciated by our spouse or our boss. Mindfulness helps us discover our real reasons for wanting to buy things. But mindfulness is not a road to pain and deprivation; rather it is about cultivating the ability to make good, nurturing, healing choices for ourselves as we move through life. For example, through the practice of mindfulness we can learn to transition from an out-of-control addiction to buying junk food, to the fully satisfying experience of eating fresh, wholesome foods. Through mindfulness we can carefully and gently see what is unfolding immediately in the present moment. This is the revolutionary path of healing that the Buddha taught.

LIVING ON AUTOMATIC PILOT

◆

Like all of us, you are a creature of habit. You create your own patterns and repetitive behaviours in response to the external world. These are your survival skills. When you were a child, you created the best patterns and habits you could in response to your parents and the environment you inherited at birth. Habits and routines can be very helpful. Having routines makes your day easier. You don't have to make a decision over every little thing.

F OR EXAMPLE, you know when to set the alarm, how long to allow for breakfast and also for the drive to work. You probably have a routine when you get there – perhaps you get your coffee, chat with your office mates for a few minutes, check your email and then get on with the day's activities. You most likely have routines for much of your day. It is all worked out for you. You can do what you have to do but be mentally elsewhere. Your mind may wander to your next holiday as you work on a report due tomorrow. It seems normal and familiar to be distracted, and you even celebrate your ability to 'multi-task'. At lunchtime you may read the paper whilst you wolf down a burger, chips and a diet soda at a fast-food restaurant, before racing back to the office.

On the drive home you may be thinking about a conversation you need to have with your partner about money. This makes you tense. The truth is the report you were working on

today could have been better. If you mindfully assessed the health consequences of eating the 'burger special' for lunch, you may have made a healthier, more satisfying choice. And the sunset on the drive home may have relaxed you in preparation for a difficult conversation – if you just would have noticed it.

We are good at living on 'automatic pilot'. We go through the motions in the present but mostly live in the past or the future. In this way we can actually miss much of our life. It is as if we are on a scenic coach tour but we keep our head in a book the whole way. We miss the beautiful sights, smells, tastes, sounds and textures that we could enjoy if we only turned our focused awareness to what is going on right now.

When it comes to your finances, being truly present in the moment may allow you to enjoy and appreciate the world around you without having the need or desire to buy anything.

With mindfulness you can learn to be satisfied and content with what you have, without feeling vulnerable to the constant pull of advertising and the societal pressure to consume. With mindfulness you can live life in a state of awareness, making decisions based on what is right for you here and now rather than responding mindlessly from outworn habits or routine.

We go through the motions in the present but mostly live in the past or the future.

LEARNING TO PAY ATTENTION

Mindfulness is the art of paying attention. Through focusing your attention on what, why and how you buy — and how you manage your financial resources — you will begin to heal your relationship with money. But first you need to learn how to focus your attention, and one way to learn this is to meditate on your breath. This very simple practice helps you learn to focus, calm your mind and be aware of the present moment.

1 Wear comfortable, loose clothing, and sit on a straight-backed chair with your feet flat on the floor. Sit slightly forwards on the chair, with your spine straight and your shoulders relaxed, without using the chair back for support. Allow your hands to rest comfortably in your lap.

2 Your head should be level and your eyes open but softly focused on a spot on the floor about 1 m (3 ft) in front of you. Make sure you are comfortable and relaxed.

3 Take a few deep breaths into your abdomen, allowing your breath to rise and fill your lungs. Breathing into your abdomen moves your diaphragm downwards, allowing your lungs to fill more easily. After a few exaggerated deep breaths continue to breathe normally into your abdomen.

4 Now simply focus on your breath itself. You can do this by focusing on the sensation of air moving over your upper lip, or you can focus on the sensation of your abdomen rising and falling, or you can simply count your breaths one to ten and then start over. Put all your attention on your breath and try to empty your mind of all thoughts. When a thought arises simply bring your attention back to your breath as you would gently and lovingly bring a small child back to your side.

5 It will be difficult to empty your mind of thoughts. And you will bring your attention back to your breath hundreds of times. But after ten minutes or so you will begin feel the calming effects of being mindful of your breath, and you will have a taste of what being present in the moment feels like. You may for example feel more aware of your body. You may miss your normal constant stream of thoughts and their attending emotions. Then again, simply focusing on your breath may release feelings of sadness or anger that you have been suppressing. Or you may simply enjoy the peace and relaxation. There is no right or wrong way to do this meditation. Simply experience it.

6 Meditate for 15 minutes or more, and when you are ready, end your meditation. In your journal write about what you experienced physically, mentally and emotionally, and what you enjoyed or found uncomfortable about the process.

MAKING GOOD DECISIONS
FOR YOURSELF

◆

When you learn to pay attention to what is happening right now, you can make better decisions for yourself and others in your care. For example, if a loved one clutches his chest and falls to the floor at dinner, it may trigger a memory of your father dying of a heart attack and leaving your mother alone and bereft. This memory may flood your mind, adding more fear to an already fearful situation. As a result you lose precious moments before you call for an ambulance. You feel paralysed, momentarily, with visions of spending your life alone without him.

MINDFULNESS IS not without emotion, but the ability to pay attention to what is going on right now without the overlay of past memories and future fears may make you more effective in dealing with many situations.

Mindfulness in your everyday life helps you to make better financial choices. With examination you may discover that some of the ways you spend your money may negatively impact your health. For example you may buy a high-fat, high-calorie, high-sugar breakfast every morning because you have grown used to it; so much so you begin to crave it. It seems impossible to start the day without stopping on the way to work for a large dose of caffeine and a sugary breakfast pastry. Your restaurant breakfasts may seem inexpensive but

they can add significantly to your monthly budget. Getting up half an hour earlier and making oatmeal, or eggs, toast and coffee in your own kitchen is a much healthier, calmer way to start the day, and a wiser decision for your budget.

Making the Transition

With the mindfulness practices you will learn, you can begin to see clearly how you allocate your money and why you spend what you do. This includes evaluating the feelings and beliefs influencing your decisions, and deciding if your financial life is in line with your personal values and financial goals. Then you can make a transition, at your own pace, to a financial plan that is congruent with how you really want to live. By practising mindfulness, you may get in touch with what you really feel and think. For example you may discover that you never really wanted to make your living as a solicitor (or salesman or construction worker) but would rather grow organic herbs on a farm and have more time with your family. Or you may decide that you do want to be a solicitor and make plans to attend law school. Then again, you may wake up to the fact that you have a great job and are grateful to have it.

Whether it is about caring for those you love, or caring for yourself, mindfulness clears away past memories and future fantasies that cloud your present experience and perception. In that clear, wise state you can make the right choices for yourself and for others.

EXERCISE 2

A MINDFUL WALK IN THE PARK

This exercise will introduce you to the practice of mindfulness as you walk in a park or nature reserve. Try this on a weekend when you can be free from the pressures of work. In this exercise you will try as best you can to avoid thinking and pay attention with intense focus to everything you are doing and experiencing.

1 Find a park or nature reserve that you would like to explore. Take a moment to breathe deeply and clear your mind of any worries or habitual thinking. Begin walking at a comfortable, leisurely pace. When your thoughts begin to wander simply bring your focus back. Pay attention to the sounds, colours and smells of everything around you. Notice the light as it filters through the trees, the temperature of the air and the feel of the breeze, if any. Pay attention to how your body feels. Is it tense or relaxed? Notice the sound of your shoes stepping on the path. Observe the movement of the birds. Avoid any tendency to speed up as you walk. Continue on at a slow, comfortable, steady pace. If this makes you nervous in any way or your thoughts begin to wander, simply take a few long slow breaths.

2 When you are ready find a place where you can be alone. Stop and listen for a few minutes and note what you hear. Can you see or hear anthing? Close your eyes and listen for animals,

birds, insects and the wind rustling in the trees. You may be aware of man-made sounds – perhaps a lawn mower or a distant road. Return your focus to the nature around you.

3 Now begin walking again and this time notice the colours around you. If it is summer notice the infinite varieties of green in the plants and trees. Perhaps there are beds of flowers, or wildflowers, or painted park benches. Note the textures – the bark of the trees, the veins of leaves and the feel of the path beneath your feet. Bring your attention to the smells – perhaps freshly mowed grass, the perfume of flowers or the pungent smell of a log rotting. When thoughts begin to take over your mind, bring your attention back. You will do this over and over again. Learning to be fully present takes practise.

4 After your walk record your thoughts and feelings about it in your journal. How was this walk different from the normal way you walk? Was it more satisfying or less? Did you feel more relaxed than usual? Did you see, hear or smell things that you normally miss? What did you like about walking mindfully? Did any emotions come up? Did you feel happy, sad, or bored? Write about how the experience made you feel and anything else that comes to mind.

5 In what ways do you feel living mindfully in the present will help you have a better financial life?

HOW TO PRACTISE
MINDFULNESS MEDITATION

◆

*Before you begin to examine your current relationship with money,
it will help you to learn the traditional mindfulness meditations on
the body, the mind and the emotions. Practising these meditations
on a daily basis will help you bring the increased self-awareness you
will enjoy to your financial life. Deepening your ability to feel and
pay attention to yourself and the world around you is essential to
exploring and healing your relationship with money.*

MINDFULNESS IS THE direct antidote to avoidance and
denial – the two most common ways people get in
trouble with their finances. Paying attention to everything
about money in your life is the most important thing you can
do to turn your financial life around. Buddhists have spent
thousands of years perfecting the art of paying attention, so
what better way to learn mindfulness than from the master
himself – the Buddha.

In the Buddhist tradition, mindfulness meditation begins
with a calm, stable mind. This state is often achieved with
meditation on the breath, which you learnt on pages 36–37.
In mindfulness meditation you work with the calm, stable
mind you have cultivated through breath meditation to investigate your body, feelings and attitudes, your mind and the
content of your thoughts, and the physical world around you.

Mindfulness is dedication to observing and seeing clearly, and being conscious and aware of what is happening in the present moment. Mindfulness helps you gain a deeper understanding of the connection between your thoughts and feelings and how they manifest in your actions related to money.

When applied to your relationship with money, mindfulness practices can be transformative. With the tools of clear focus and stable concentration you begin to observe yourself and see who you are, how you act, what you feel and what you think when it comes to finances. Through mindfulness you begin to know yourself in a deeper way. The fog of unconsciousness lifts and it becomes easier to make good choices for yourself, so that handling your finances becomes a healthy, supportive, pleasurable activity.

The Power to Change

Mindfulness meditation leads naturally to examination of things you may think of as fixed such as your personality, your ideas about money and your habits around spending. You may think of these aspects of yourself as unchangeable, even though obviously you have changed and evolved over time since you were a child. Not realising you have the ability to change, you may continue on each day trapped in habitual thoughts and behaviours around money that are not serving you. Through mindfulness practices, you can begin to recognise your patterns and perhaps choose better alternatives.

MINDFULNESS OF YOUR BODY

◆

Some spiritual traditions teach that you must ignore the body and move towards a more spiritual approach to life where you identify exclusively with the mind. The body may be considered as defiled and a source of 'sin', to be neglected and ignored. It may be that negative feelings about money and ignoring body sensations may have its roots in some of these traditions. Yet we are incarnated in a human body. It enables us to communicate, to work, to love, to experience joy, to eat, to sleep and to take care of ourselves.

RATHER THAN BEING an enemy our bodies are a source of pleasure, joy, inspiration and spiritual development. Through our bodies we appreciate the world around us. It is important to learn to pay attention to our bodies, to care for them well, and to stay in balance physically and mentally as much as possible. Becoming mindful of this beautiful instrument that is our body will help us reconnect if we have been split off from our physical sensations through trauma or abuse.

Becoming Aware

Since the body and mind are not separate, awareness of the body also provides a window into our psychological states. The pain in the neck, the tensed jaw, the tightness in the chest, the lack of feeling in the groin area may point to areas of our psyche that need exploration and healing. Overspending is

easy to do if you are cut off from feeling your body fully. Focusing closely on your body will help you release areas of armouring you may not have been aware of, and open you to moving through the psychological blocks they may represent. For example you may have unexpressed or even unacknowledged sadness because your parents were not very nurturing when you were a child. That sadness takes up residence in your body, perhaps in the form of excess weight, because you may be turning to food to fill the emptiness inside. And you may be trying to replace the love you missed by buying expensive clothes, shoes or furniture to make yourself feel special. By releasing physical and psychological blocks you can begin to normalise and heal your relationship with money. When you begin to be more in touch with your body and your emotions, they will help you decide if a purchase is a good idea or not, if a job is right for you, or if this is the right house to buy.

> It's also helpful to realise that this very body that we have, that's sitting right here right now... with its aches and it pleasures... is exactly what we need to be fully human, fully awake, fully alive.
>
> PEMA CHÖDRÖN

BODY MINDFULNESS EXERCISE

Set aside about 30 minutes for this exercise, choosing a time when you can be alone and undisturbed. If possible, record the instructions for this exercise so that you can play them back to yourself.

1 Sit on a straight-backed chair with both feet on the floor and your hands resting in your lap. Sit a little forwards on the seat. You should feel upright but relaxed, as if a string attached to the top of your head is holding you up from above.

2 With your eyes closed or slightly open, relax any tense areas of your body and calm your mind by focusing on your breath for a few minutes.

3 Now shift your focus to your feet. Feel your feet firmly on the ground, and make sure they are relaxed. Be aware of any physical sensations and relax any tensions that may be present. Then move your awareness to your ankles and lower legs and do the same. Next move your awareness to your knees, then to your thighs. Do you notice any tightness, burning, tingling or an ache? Is it constant or changing? Try to focus completely on any sensation whilst remaining neutral and detached. Just be aware. If there is pain simply note that there is pain. When thoughts intrude, bring your awareness back.

4 Now move to your groin area and stomach area. Relax and let your breath fill your lower abdomen. Breathe into your lower abdomen for a minute or two, then move your awareness into your mid and upper chest area.

5 Next focus on your neck, letting go of any tension in this area. When ready move your attention to your face. Relax every part of your face – your mouth, eyes, jaw and forehead.

6 Move your attention to more subtle sensations. Focus for a few minutes on your heart beating in your chest. Then expand your awareness to your veins and arteries connecting to your heart, and try to feel the blood pumping through them.

7 Focus on the general feeling of energy moving through your body. Feel energy moving around your spine, through your torso and in your groin area. Stay with neutral observation, avoiding labelling anything positive or negative.

8 Shift your attention to your senses. What are you seeing, tasting, or smelling at this moment? What colours do you notice? Pay attention to what you hear. Simply listen carefully to the sounds near and far, as well as the sound of your breath.

9 Return to focusing on your breath and meditate for a few minutes before ending this exercise.

Body Mindfulness & Finances

What does this body mindfulness exercise have to do with your finances? Often when you have trouble with money in your life you have cut off feelings in your body. When you begin to practise feeling your body again you can begin to distinguish a healthy purchase from a neurotic one. You will be more aware of when you are tense or anxious, and instead of unconsciously trying to ease your tension by buying clothes you can't afford, you can address your emotional needs directly by keeping a journal, exercising, taking a bath or calling a friend. You can begin to undo any body armouring from old physical or emotional wounds that may be causing you to overspend or impulsively buy things that you think will make you feel better about yourself, and erase the shame that haunts you from your past.

Your body is as intelligent as your mind, and it has a lot to tell you about what is happening in this very moment – both around and inside you. But you won't know that unless you let it speak to you. By practising mindfulness of the body you will learn to hear the messages it wants to send to you – especially when you spend money. By acknowledging your body's message you can let your body, as well as your mind, guide your life.

Practise mindfulness of the body when you are feeling disconnected with your body, having trouble with managing your finances or taking care of yourself physically, or if you

simply want to experience your body in a new and beneficial way. After spending some time closely attending to your body in mindfulness meditation you can bring this attention

> Human happiness and human satisfaction must ultimately come from within oneself. It is wrong to expect some final satisfaction to come from money or from a computer.
>
> TENZIN GYATSO, 14TH DALAI LAMA

to your body in daily life. You can extend your body awareness in doing everyday activities such as walking, eating, speaking, driving and observing the world through your senses. By paying close attention to your body you will learn more about your physical patterns and habits, change those that are harmful or negative, be conscious of subtle changes that may indicate illness, and be better able to maintain your health and well-being. You will begin to know when you are hungry, and when you have eaten enough for your body's needs. You will know if you really need to buy something, or if you are just feeling down. You will get in touch with how you feel at your job, and if it is the right one for you.

MINDFULNESS OF YOUR EMOTIONS

◆

In practising mindfulness of emotions, it helps to explore how emotions come into being. First we have some kind of sensory stimulus or thought that becomes a basis for a feeling to arise. For example, your partner arrives home early from work and you experience pleasure at seeing him or her, or you have an immediate sense of fear because you know there are redundancies in the offing. Or you may feel fear because things have not been going well between you.

FEELINGS AND ATTITUDES often are a stimulus to action. Pleasure at seeing your partner may lead you to invite him or her to sit down and have a cup of coffee and talk. If you feel a threat you may let him stand there and be uncomfortable until you know why he is home early. If anger arises you may say something you regret. Usually the whole sequence of events – a feeling that gives rise to an attitude (or vice versa) or to an action – is experienced seamlessly, and feels a part of us and our identity.

The Impulse Buy

If you are used to impulsively buying something when you feel any strong emotion, you may do so in a similar seamless fashion – without even thinking. For example, if your partner loses his job, in the days that follow you may order some items from a catalogue because you don't want to face the reality

that your income was just reduced significantly. And if he just got off early and nothing terrible happened, out of relief you may suggest that you go out to dinner at an expensive restaurant even though you have significant credit card debt.

Observing Your Emotions

Through mindfulness meditation you can learn to pay close attention to your feelings and avoid any tendency to repress or suppress them. There is nothing wrong with your emotions. The problem is when you identify strongly with a particular emotional state. For example, you may think 'I am angry' or 'I am depressed' rather than removing the 'I' and acknowledging that yes, 'there is anger, there is sadness', or 'there is fear'. Through practising mindfulness you can begin to observe your anger or your fear (or any other emotion) without judgement. You will learn that emotions arise, linger and pass away, and that you don't have to get caught up in them, or compulsively express them in a way that may be destructive to yourself or others. With awareness you can avoid spending time or energy to push feelings down or take away any pain you may be feeling. Whatever you are feeling represents a snapshot of where you are at this moment and those feelings often change over time.

EMOTIONS MINDFULNESS EXERCISE

For this exercise you will need a straight-backed chair. Ensure you are sitting comfortably without using the back of the chair for support.

1 Begin by focusing on your breath for a few minutes to calm and clear your mind.

2 Choose a personal situation or a person you know to be your focus for this exercise. Create in your mind a vivid mental image of this situation or person with as much detail as possible. As you contemplate the image, let any feelings arise and note what attitude accompanies them. It is OK if your attitude is positive or negative. Try not to judge yourself.

3 Shift your attention to your emotional state connected to this situation or person. How do you feel about it (or him or her) this moment? Are you happy, sad, afraid or angry? Try to watch your emotional state as an observer without identifying with it.

4 If your emotional state is pleasant try not to cling to it. If you are sad try not to push it away. Remind yourself how often your emotional state shifts and how many emotions you have experienced and moved through. Meditate on the fact that all emotional states are impermanent and transitory.

Unacknowledged emotions can undermine your financial life. Becoming mindful and aware of your emotions is a first step to intervening in an unhealthy relationship with money. Checking yourself on a regular basis to assess your emotional state will help you rein in impulsive spending, or other ways you have a negative relationship to money. Acknowledge whatever you are feeling, and instead of turning to the credit card choose a creative way to address your emotions and whatever is bothering you such as writing in your journal or talking to a friend. If you are angry or upset ask yourself why you feel that way. If you are sad or lonely write about what triggered those feelings. The simple act of acknowledging your feelings can be enough to ward off an unwise purchase. Remind yourself that everything is impermanent – including your emotions.

We feel money and power can bring happiness and solve problems, but they are not definite causes of those desired states. If that were so it would follow that those who have wealth would necessarily have happiness, and those who do not have wealth would always experience suffering. Money and power facilitate, but it is clear that they are not the primary causes of happiness and solving our problems.

TENZIN GYATSO, 14TH DALAI LAMA

MINDFULNESS OF YOUR MIND

◆

We have explored mindfulness of the body and of emotions or feelings. Now we will look at the third mindfulness, that of the mind. Here we are working directly with the contents of the mind itself – thoughts, mental images, perceptions, emotions, feelings, memories, fantasies and desires as they arise and fall away in a continuous stream.

As you have discovered in this chapter, your mind, in its normal state, is somewhat out of control. The chaos of mental activity that takes over your daily life is actually a kind of dream state that is divorced from direct experience of reality. Like most people, you live by habit and routine through much of the day. Through mindfulness of your thoughts, you can learn to bring yourself into the present. This will help you make better decisions about how to manage your money.

You begin by simply observing your thoughts as they enter your awareness and then disappear. You try not to identify with them or get carried away by any one thought. Then instead of simply watching them, you observe patterns in the content. Is there an emotional tone that repeats such as fear or anger? Do your thoughts seem to drift to money, health, food or sex? Are you either planning for the future or reliving memories? By examining your thoughts you can begin to consciously choose their contents, replacing negative neurotic thinking patterns with more wholesome and productive ones.

EXERCISE 5

MIND MINDFULNESS EXERCISE

You will need a straight-backed chair to sit on. Refer to the previous mindfulness exercises for directions on how to sit.

1 Begin by simply observing your breath for a few minutes to calm and clear your mind.

2 Now begin to observe your thoughts as they enter your awareness and then disappear. Try not to identify with or get carried away by any one thought. Simply observe the content of your thoughts. Perhaps you are thinking about meditation, work, your loved ones or the film you saw last night.

3 After a few minutes begin to observe patterns in the content. Notice any emotional tone such as fear or anger. Do your thoughts drift to money, health or work? Are you imagining the worst is going to happen? Accept whatever thought arises.

4 Observe that by noticing your thoughts you have become more conscious of them. This gives you a tool for noticing neurotic thinking patterns that negatively affect your financial life. If you find yourself constantly worrying about the future, take a moment to breathe into the worry. Consider that in this present moment there is nothing to fear.

Developing Awareness

As you become more aware of your thoughts, you will begin to notice which ones bring more happiness and peace and which ones bring more pain and stress. Thoughts of generosity, kindness and joy have different effects than thoughts of greed, fear, anger and aversion. As you investigate your different thought patterns and mind-states, let yourself experience deeply what they are like. If you tend to be judgemental it will become apparent to you that being judgemental causes your own pain and misery. If you are tolerant and accepting you will begin to see that the mind-states of tolerance and acceptance are a prerequisite to unconditional love. Through practising mindfulness of the mind you become aware of how your thoughts create your experience, and how they determine your happiness.

Your Thoughts Shape Your Life

Learning to pay attention to the content of your thoughts as you go about your day will help you gain control of your life and move it in a positive direction. With practise you will begin to identify the thought patterns that cause you difficulty with money and other aspects of your life. If you tend to have jealous thoughts when others get ahead, try rejoicing in others' good fortune. If you tend to think of yourself as a failure, instead of dwelling on your negatives spend time listing everything you have accomplished in your life – even the

smallest victories are worth celebrating. If you think you have no skills or talent, make a list in your journal of everything you can do. If you are a good cook write it down. Your thoughts shape your life, so spending time being mindful of them will help you manifest the life you want.

Making a habit of being mindful – of your body, what you think and what you feel – will transform your life. It's not that by practising mindfulness all your money problems will disappear: that would be unrealistic because who knows what the future will bring. But armed with the excellent tool of mindfulness you will be able to navigate your financial life with more clarity and ease.

> It's only when we truly know and understand that we have a limited time on earth – and that we have no way of knowing when our time is up – we will then begin to live each day to the fullest, as if it was the only one we had.
>
> ELIZABETH KUBLER-ROSS

PART II

YOUR RELATIONSHIP WITH MONEY

*Money is one of the most powerful aspects of your life,
yet you are not alone if you have trouble managing it.
You may avoid looking at your finances or keeping your
account from going into overdraft. It's not that you are
incapable of doing these things. You may manage money
brilliantly for the company you work for, but when it
comes to your own finances you struggle. By becoming
mindful and aware of the positive and negative aspects
of your current relationship with money you can release
yourself from any guilt and shame from the past,
and bring your financial life in alignment with
your highest values and deepest needs.*

WHAT YOUR FAMILY
TAUGHT YOU ABOUT MONEY

When we were children our impressionable minds picked up all sorts of ideas about what money is and how it works. Some of these ideas were the accidental misunderstandings of a childish mind. Others were lessons learnt from our parents' less than ideal habits and attitudes towards money. And of course, adding to the confusion, we also received some good advice. So, you may make a lot of money, as your parents advised you to do, but you may be a poor manager of what you have, as they may have been.

YOUR PARENTS MAY HAVE EXPRESSED their love by giving you expensive gifts, rather than affection – their presents not quite making up for that hole in your heart. They may have insisted that you wear expensive clothes, so you learnt that appearances are everything; more important than what kind of person you are or what you feel. Their motivation may have been to make you happy and secure but their messages were mixed and confusing. By becoming mindful of these messages you can release their hold on you.

Becoming mindful of the money messages you learnt as a child gives you an opportunity to see which are serving you and which are holding you back, which to keep and which to discard. You may discover the ideas and beliefs you have about money are not really yours at all, but are family heirlooms.

MONEY MEMORIES EXERCISE

1 Find a time when you can be alone and undisturbed. Using your Mindfulness Budget journal, write down your earliest memories about money. You may recall something you wanted that failed to materialise. Perhaps your family was well-off and you never thought about what anything cost. Your grandmother may have told you that money will not buy you happiness.

2 Write down how you felt about money as a child and who influenced those feelings. As you got older did the messages or your views about money change? Does recalling your family messages bring up feelings of shame or guilt? Are you happy and grateful for what your parents taught you about money?

3 Spend about an hour on this exercise. Consider if and how the messages from the past are affecting your financial life today. Write down the money messages that have most influenced you. Decide if you want to continue to live by these messages or create new ones that fit more with who you are today.

4 For messages you feel no longer serve you, write an antidote. If you learnt that money is evil, or that people who have money are bad, write an antidote that money can be a force for good, and that a wealthy person can be kind and compassionate.

WHAT THE WORLD
TELLS YOU ABOUT MONEY

◆

There is no doubt that the world tells you — through peer pressure, advertising and other cultural influences — to value money first above everything else. Global advertising is poised to surpass £300 billion per year. Being bombarded by advertising on a daily basis makes it difficult to resist the message that money and possessions will make you happy. You are pulled not only to buy objects such as cars, clothes or cosmetics, but also to buy joy and serenity, love, youth, and a body different than the one you have — all of which of course can't be bought.

THERE IS THE temptation to get caught in a vicious circle. You may go into debt buying things you can't afford — in order to appear more powerful and successful, attract a high paying job, or pay off your debt. Becoming mindful of what the world is telling you about money gives you a chance to decide yourself what you want your relationship with money to be, and how you really want to live your life.

The Midas Touch

In the Greek myth everything King Midas touched turned to gold. Yet his ability to turn everything into money became a devastating curse. Like Midas, too many of us value things that have a price tag and devalue those that do not. Working overtime to afford a powerboat or a kitchen makeover becomes more important than loving moments spent with close family and friends. An executive director's highly compensated work seems more valuable than a nurse's or a teacher's or a mother's work caring for her children. The world tells us – through peer pressure, advertising and other cultural influences – to value money and things above all else.

Questioning the world's preoccupation with money opens us to the infinite joys to be had in any moment. It can make us less vulnerable to advertising and less likely to confuse material wealth with emotional and spiritual fulfilment. Advertising tells us that a new sports car will give us power, sexual attractiveness and confidence. A perfume ad promises us romance and intimacy. But the car cannot fill that hole of insecurity, fear and longing, and the perfume will not deliver lifelong happiness with the man of our dreams.

Midas Sees the Light

King Midas 'bought' what the world told him about money – that it was more important than anything else, and that he could never have enough. When the gods granted his wish to have everything he touched turn to gold, he accidentally touched his daughter, and she turned into a gold statue before his eyes. He immediately felt the pain and loss of a world without love and intimacy, and the joy of sensual and spiritual experience. Luckily, he was able to have his wished reversed.

EXERCISE 7

MONEY MESSAGES EXERCISE

The following exercise is similar to the previous one. But this time you are drawing not on memory but rather on your present life. Becoming mindful of the messages the world tells you is the beginning of taking back control of your financial life. Instead of living a life based on assumptions you can begin to decide for yourself how you want to live when it comes to money – or anything else.

1 Find a time when you can be undisturbed for about an hour. Begin to list what society tells you about money. For example, you may write that society tells you that money is the most important thing in the world, or that having a lot of money means you can have whatever you want or anyone you wish for. You may believe what society and the media tells you – that money really does buy happiness. Whatever you feel are the general messages of the world around you about money, write them down. Don't worry if they sound extreme. If you came up with them then they must be out there in some fashion.

2 If you are at college, list the messages that come from your teachers and fellow students. If you are working, draw your list from your managers and co-workers. As an adult, your spouse, parents, siblings or grandparents may still have a significant influence over how you think about your financial life. Your close friends will share their opinions about money and the meaning of success. Write down the money messages you have received from the important people in your life.

3 If you attend church, members of your congregation and your minister may impart subtle or direct messages about money. Money may be a source of evil, or conversely its accumulation a symbol of virtue and hard work. Write about what you have learnt.

4 TV, advertising, magazines and the Internet can exert a heavy influence on how you think about money and on what you choose to consume. What general messages have you absorbed from these sources?

5 Now decide which of those messages you feel are right for you and which are in conflict with who you are or the person you want to be.

6 For those messages you have difficulty with write a counter message that fits your values and who you are. If you feel society wrongly puts a price tag on everything then counter that with a list of things that cannot be bought. If you feel that excessive competition for money is harming the world or the environment write about how less competition and more sharing could help the planet.

YOUR MONEY FANTASIES

If you have a 9 to 5 job you have probably imagined what it would be like to live in luxury without having to work. Perhaps you have watched a TV game show where contestants compete to become millionaires, and vicariously shared in the thrill of the win. Maybe you have imagined winning the lottery and retiring to an island villa in the sun. But if fantasies and daydreams about wealth are a recurrent theme in your thinking they may be preventing you from dealing with your current financial reality. You may be using fantasies to avoid facing your fears about money, and distract you from taking action to improve your financial life.

I MAGINING OR VISUALISING what you want in your future is an important first step to making it happen. But there is a difference between creative imagination that is based in reality and living in a fantasy world. The first is an important tool in manifesting the life you want, and the latter is a way to avoid dealing with reality.

Facing Your Fantasies

In your Mindfulness Budget journal write down any fantasies you may have that you feel may be contributing to your financial problems. For example, you may imagine marrying a wealthy man or woman as a way to solve your debt problems, or avoid having to manage your money or make a living.

Deep down you want someone else to take care of those things for you. Or you may have an addiction to gambling. Even though you are sinking deeper in debt you imagine that soon you will have a big win, and all your problems will be over. Many people buy the occasional lottery ticket, but you may imagine that if you spend a lot of money on lottery tickets every week you are bound to win, and all your problems will evaporate.

> If you live for having it all what you have is never enough. In an environment of more is better 'enough' is like the horizon – always receding. You lose the ability to identify that point of sufficiency at which you can choose to stop.
>
> JOE DOMINGUEZ

Through writing down your financial fantasies you are bringing them into your awareness. You are using a mindfulness exercise to confront mental states and behaviours that are holding you back from real financial peace and stability. Most importantly you are doing so with caring and compassion. When you have admitted your fantasies to yourself you can stop using them to avoid your financial reality. You can begin to live in the present and directly face your financial fears.

EXERCISE 8

FINANCIAL FEARS EXERCISE

Financial fears can be overwhelming, but by practising mindfulness you can begin to face them. You can decide which fears are based in reality and which stem from your propensity to worry. Using mindfulness to identify fearful emotions related to money and finances, and then doing something constructive to address them, is one of the most empowering things you can do for yourself.

1 Find an hour when you can be alone and undisturbed and take a few minutes to relax and focus on working with your fears. Remember that the purpose of becoming mindful of your fears is not to torture yourself, or judge yourself, or frighten yourself further, but to face them directly and gain some relief.

2 Using your Mindfulness Budget journal make a list and write about your financial fears. Be open and direct in describing the money issues that scare you. If you feel tightness in your body or find you are holding your breath, take a moment to breathe deeply. Be sure to list the smaller fears as well as the big ones. For example, you may be afraid your friend will not want your company if you choose not to go to expensive restaurants. A more pressing fear may be that because your car broke down and you cannot afford the repair you have no way to get to work. You may even unearth some hidden fears. For example, you may discover that deep down you fear your in-laws look down on you and your family for not being as well off or that, because you have no children you fear getting old and having no one to take care of you.

3 When you feel you have recorded every financial fear you are aware of take a moment to congratulate yourself. Facing fears directly takes courage.

4 Now go back and choose an action that will address each fear. For example, if your friend's choice in restaurants is breaking your budget do some research to find some well-reviewed but less expensive restaurants and suggest you try those instead. If the looming car repair bill is scaring you explore getting a ride to work, or taking public transportation, until you can save up enough to have the car repaired. If there is a real chance you may be made redundant begin to update your CV and explore other job possibilities.

5 If, for no real reason, you tend to worry about losing your job take a look at your fear and see what is behind it. Perhaps it is an expression of low self-esteem. If so, try self-help books, attending a workshop or seeing a counsellor. Taking action to address any psychological issues you find behind your financial fears will help you feel more balanced and less anxious.

EXERCISE 9

COPING WITH FINANCIAL STRESS EXERCISE

Ongoing financial stress can negatively affect your emotional life, causing anxiety, depression and insomnia. The following exercise brings mindful awareness to your financial stress and how you cope with it. You can begin relieving financial stress right now by choosing healthier ways of coping. Finding positive ways to cope now will help you create a more positive relationship with money going forwards.

1 Sit in a quiet place where you can be undisturbed. Breathe deeply and slowly into your abdomen until you feel centred and fully present in your body.

2 Bring to mind the areas in your life of financial stress and difficulty. You may think of your credit card bills, disagreements with your partner over money, problems with managing your current account, concerns about keeping your job or advancing in your career. If there are specific issues bring those up as well – perhaps an expensive, overdue car repair or home repair is on your mind.

3 Notice how thinking about money makes you feel. Do you feel angry, fearful, anxious or nervous? Do you feel hopeless or ashamed? Notice the ways in which your emotional life is affected by money. Are you in a constant state of worry, or do you find yourself snapping at the children or your partner for no reason? Bring your attention to your body and note how thinking about money affects your facial expression, tension in your jaw, your muscles and your breathing.

4 Now bring to mind the ways you cope with the emotions that arise from financial stress. You may be coping by drinking too much, smoking or overeating. Maybe you ignore your family and friends. Or, though broke, you cope by going shopping. Or perhaps you turn to meditation and prayer. Where do you stand in coping with your financial stress? Simply note what you do without being judgemental or critical. Think about what really helps and what doesn't when financial stress overtakes you.

5 Close your eyes and breathe deeply and slowly for a minute. Breathe in peace and calm in the form of golden light, and breathe out any tension in your body in the form of dark smoke.

6 When you are ready, open your eyes. In your Mindfulness Budget journal write down five beneficial ways to cope when you feel stress about money. When the credit card bills are due and you feel fear and worry taking over choose to take a brisk walk, a hot bath or a cup of calming herbal tea. Or try meditating on your breath until you feel calmer and ready to face what is in front of you. Make a payment and congratulate yourself that you are on the path to financial freedom.

GUILT, SHAME & REGRET

You are not alone if you have aspects of your financial past you would rather others did not know. Perhaps ten years ago you inherited some money from your great aunt, but instead of saving or investing it you spent it on a very expensive, luxurious holiday. Today, because you are in serious debt, you regret that you were so short-sighted. Alternatively, perhaps you impulsively bought a house that looked lovely and seemed a bargain, but because it had serious structural deficiencies you had to sell it at a loss.

PERHAPS YOU had a problem with substance abuse and harmed your family by spending money that should have gone for their support. Or you had been addicted to shopping and maxed out several credit cards. Then there was that stock-market tip that sounded too good to be true – because it was.

Even if you were a victim of fraud you may suffer from feelings of guilt, shame or regret. Perhaps a contractor took your money and disappeared without doing the work, and you feel guilty because you neglected to review his background thoroughly. Even very wealthy people who are very savvy about money have been victims of investment fraud. In a recent case in New York investors who gave their money to a swindler named Bernie Madoff lost millions – because they ignored the fact that the returns on their investment were 'too good to be true'.

EXERCISE 10

FORGIVING MISTAKES EXERCISE

Having guilt, shame or regret about past financial mistakes is only human. Like everyone, you imagine you are rational with money, but in reality you are swayed by advertising, your emotions and the influence of others. Having regret is an appropriate response, as it will help you avoid the same mistakes in the future. But having guilt and shame is holding you back. Bringing up your past mistakes can help you replace these useless emotions with compassion and forgiveness.

1 Find a time when you can be alone. In your Mindfulness Budget journal list every financial mistake you can remember from your childhood until the present.

2 After each mistake take a moment to forgive yourself. Visualise the money you lost or the objects you bought – and the guilt and shame attached to them – rising in the air like a balloon and disappearing over the horizon. Sell the objects or give them away to someone who may need them. Mentally and emotionally let go of the money you no longer have.

3 With the past behind you, visualise a door opening and true abundance entering your life. Armed with a new attitude of self-love and self-acceptance, you can move forwards without the emotional baggage of the past.

EXERCISE 11

FINANCIAL SECRETS EXERCISE

Financial mistakes are one thing, but do you have financial secrets? Truth-telling can be scary and painful, even if it is only to ourselves. Yet releasing the burden of your financial secrets is one of the best things you can do to heal your relationship with money.

1 Compose a letter to the person you would least like to know about your financial secrets. Think of any aspects of your financial life that you would not want the person to know. It could involve something unethical or illegal such as theft, fraud or embezzlement. Whatever it is, simply let the person know about your financial secrets and how you feel about them.

2 Do not send the letter. Simply owning this truth will bring relief. Generate a sense of compassion for yourself and your struggles with money, along with a strong sense of regret for whatever you have done. When you are ready, burn the letter and imagine the fire purifying the negativity in your past.

3 Now decide on an antidote action for each secret. If you stole money in the past give the same amount to charity. If you took something without consent return it to the owner, anonymously if you wish. If you have been altering your records for tax purposes stop doing it.

Bringing Mindful Awareness
to Your Financial Situation

◆

Using your Mindfulness Budget journal spend an hour or so writing about how you are doing financially. Concentrate on the big picture more than the details. Take as much time as you need. Describe what is going well and what is not. Perhaps you make a decent income and you enjoy your work, but you don't know where the money goes. In addition you may have accumulated significant debt on your credit cards. Or it may be that you hate your job and wish you could afford to do something else.

Perhaps you and your partner have disagreements about how to spend money and different goals for the future. Or you feel you *should* have certain things in life that match your identity – your sense of who you are – but they are beyond your means.

On the other hand, you may not be making enough money, and things are so bad you may have to move in with your parents. Sometimes it is difficult to know if you are over-spending or under-earning. If you are having difficulty paying *basic* expenses such as a low- to mid-range rent or mortgage, transportation to work, groceries and utilities, then you may need to explore ways to increase your income – such as learning a new skill or applying for a better job – or share expenses with someone until you can do so. You may have

issues with self-esteem that you need to address, or ideas you learnt from your parents or others that are holding you back and merit exploration. Try to be as honest and clear-headed as you can be in describing your financial situation today.

Managing Your Money

In Part III you will explore how to mindfully manage your money in specific ways, but reflecting on how you feel and think about your current financial situation is where you start. If you are afraid or angry about money write about it. If you feel financially unstable and worried about your future write about how your situation affects you on a day-to-day basis. If you feel confused and inept when it comes to managing your money write down, in general, the ways you have problems. Perhaps you are not clear about how much you make after taxes or how much you owe. Simply describing your current financial situation to yourself will help ground you in the present, and help you identify the overall issues you need to address to improve your relationship with money.

MONEY, TIME & VALUES

◆

You are not alone if the life you live is in conflict with the values you hold dear. In your mind you may truly believe that family and friends are more important than money. Yet you may work long hours at a demanding high-paying job so that you achieve a standard of living you feel you, your spouse and children should have.

To keep that job you may bring work home and have less time in the evenings and at weekends. Your commute may be long and your clothing expensive so you can look the part. You drive an expensive car because you want to appear to be an up and coming professional, married to an equally successful spouse. You live in a beautiful home that you can barely afford. Your credit card may be maxed out, but you imagine things will straighten out when you get that next promotion. You have a high-paying job, but the cost of having that job – the expensive suits, the fancy house and car, the long commute – may mean that your hourly wage is much less than you think.

What Price are You Willing to Pay?

Our time on earth is limited. Although we imagine living a long life we don't really know when it will end. And even if we live a long life, the older we get the faster it seems to go by. So, the important question to ask yourself is: how do I

want to spend my time? More specifically, how much of my precious time am I willing to spend making a living? When I buy something how much of my life energy am I willing to expend making the money to pay for it?

Find some time to be alone and undisturbed and in your Mindfulness Budget journal write about what you value most in life. What are those things, activities and people that mean the most to you? For example, you may love, more than anything, spending time with your spouse and children. Perhaps you enjoy cooking for friends, growing roses or camping in the countryside. Or, you may find volunteering with troubled youth in your neighbourhood deeply rewarding.

Although you may never be a world-class concert violinist or a famous artist, you may love to play in your community orchestra or paint watercolours. The earth and the environment may be very important to you, and you would prefer to live in a more environmentally conscious way than you do. How can you do all these things and still make a living?

Achieving Balance

If you are living a lifestyle in which many of the experiences, things, and people you love and value are missing from your life, then it is time to reassess exactly how you use your time and how you spend your money. Begin by paying attention to your values and trying to incorporate them into your life now. For example, you could schedule an outing with your children, or have your friends over for dinner. All of life, as you know, is a balancing act. If you feel stressed

and dissatisfied with your current life you may need to rebalance to bring your life in alignment with your values and needs. If so, take some time to ask yourself what you are willing to change to make that happen. Are you willing to live a simpler lifestyle, move to a smaller home, have a less stressful, lower-paying job, but perhaps a more enjoyable life? Are you willing to give up status for doing more of what you love? Can you find balance by letting go of your workaholic tendencies? Would simply spending less and using your time more wisely allow you to live in alignment with your deepest needs and highest values?

Take Your Time

There is no rush. This exercise can be ongoing as thoughts come to you. Making changes in how you live and work takes time. Being mindful of what you really feel and think requires thoughtful reflection on alternatives, as well as consultation with those whose lives would be impacted. And of course every solution to balancing values and making a living is highly personal. There are no right or wrong choices. If you commit to living your life in accordance with your deepest needs and highest aspirations you will have a strong foundation for building your Mindfulness Budget.

CONSUMERISM & THE EARTH

◆

Our planet has suffered from our addiction to burning oil and coal, both of which have contributed to global warming. We manufacture with abandon toxic chemicals that poison the earth and turn large swathes of our oceans into dead zones. An area of the Pacific Ocean collects waterborne rubbish because of the low wind and circular currents. According to some estimates, this growing rubbish collection is now twice the size of the US state of Texas.

THE DEBRIS ranges in size from giant nets to tiny pieces of plastic. In fact, in this area, the tiny pieces of plastic are so prevalent that there is an estimated six times more plastic than plankton. Unfortunately, small fish are eating the debris instead of plankton. Larger pieces of plastic kill birds that try to eat it, or wrap around mammals, fish and sea turtles, harming and/or disfiguring them.

In addition a growing mountain of discarded mobile phones and computers containing toxic elements pollutes Third World countries where they are shipped to be 'recycled'. The over-consumption of beef contributes greatly to global warming and the pollution of our rivers and streams. The 2010 oil spill in the Gulf of Mexico, caused by deep-water drilling, is a reminder of how our addiction to oil is damaging the planet and its delicate ecosystems. The list is endless when it comes to how we are harming the earth with our endless consumption.

What We Buy Matters

This depressing litany is not meant to make you feel hopeless or guilty. The culture we live in makes it extremely difficult to rein in our consumption or sort out what is healthy to consume and what is not. We are profoundly connected to everyone and everything on the planet. What we buy matters, as everything has an effect on the health of the planet.

Educating yourself about the 'green' movement and products that are less harmful to the earth will help you spend money in a more mindful and enlightened way – and will be a more healthy choice for the earth. If more of us become mindful of the consequences of our consumption and make better choices, collectively our actions can make a difference.

Making a Difference

As you go about your daily life you contribute to the greenhouse gas emissions that are causing climate change. How you travel to work, what you eat, how you power your home and what you consume and throw in the rubbish, all influence your carbon footprint. Striving to lower your carbon emissions can help ensure a stable climate for future generations.

In a computer search engine, type in the term 'carbon footprint calculator' to help you determine how many tonnes of carbon dioxide and other greenhouse gases your choices create each year. This tool will help you be more mindful of how your consumption affects the earth.

WEALTH, SCARCITY & ABUNDANCE

In modern culture money is synonymous with wealth. But a better definition of wealth is not the accumulation of money but rather the experience of abundance. The scarcity principle teaches us that wealth is money and material things, resources are limited, and there is not enough to go around. So life becomes a competition — for professional positions, income, social status and the newest 'must have' electronic device.

THE SCARCITY PRINCIPLE drives contemporary economies and fuels the cycle of supply and demand. Low supply of an item, coupled with a high demand pushed by advertising, creates a scarcity that raises the price, making it more expensive and sought after. Marketing and advertising strategies try to capitalise on and promote the scarcity principle because it works. By creating fear of an imminent shortage, advertising creates a demand that benefits company sales but has a negative effect on people and society. When a new software operating system is released, many camp out the night before to make sure they get a copy before it sells out. Sadly, when a new popular toy is released near the holiday season, people have been trampled in the rush to buy one. How many times have you heard 'Sale price effective through Saturday only! Get yours whilst it lasts!'?

The Scarcity Mindset

The scarcity principle, rooted in greed and competition, encourages fear and selfish behaviour. It defines wealth as the accumulation and hoarding of money and things. The underlying assumption is the more you have the better off you are. One of the worst effects of the scarcity mindset is that it discourages you from sharing ideas, opportunities and resources out of a fear that someone will steal from you. If you view life through the lens of scarcity, sadly even your closest friend's success may be felt as your loss. Scarcity makes you afraid that someone having more than you do, being more successful than you are or achieving more than you have lowers your worth and value. It is often at the root of low self-esteem.

The Abundance Principle

In contrast, the abundance principle assumes there is more than enough to go around for everyone. Based firmly in the Buddha's realisation of impermanence, the abundance principle sees the world as continually creating new opportunities and fresh challenges. The mind of abundance believes that there is room for everyone to benefit, and that the more you share the more you receive in return. By being generous to others you will attract the generosity of others; by helping others you will receive help in return, and by giving out of a sense of abundance you will always have what you need. It is the Buddha's law of karma in action.

On the other hand acting out of scarcity causes you to turn inwards and focus on yourself, stifling the happiness that comes from generosity – the joy of giving and sharing. When you act from the mind of abundance you will be happy to take only what you need and share the rest. In the abundance mindset you strive to benefit yourself and everyone around you. You realise that your happiness is dependent on others' happiness. Your life takes on a greater purpose and meaning than just looking after yourself and those closest to you.

Wealth is More Than Money

From a position of abundance there is room for everyone, opportunities are limitless, and creativity abounds. The scarcity principle is based on fear and greed, which causes no end of psychological stress; the abundance principle is built on faith and equality and induces relaxation in mind and body. Where the scarcity principle demands hoarding, the abundance principle promotes sharing and the valuing of people and experience over money and possessions.

From the viewpoint of abundance, wealth is much more than money and possessions. The majority of your wealth comes from your relationships, your experiences, your education, your health and your spiritual understanding. Expressing gratitude for all that you have and have been given relieves the stress of feeling that you never have enough. Seeing the world as full of abundance relieves your fear of losing it all.

EXERCISE 12

PRACTISING GRATITUDE EXERCISE

Becoming mindful of your wealth in all its forms, and expressing gratitude for it on a daily basis, is one of the best practices for healing your relationship with money. This practice can be as short or long as you like. Consider practising gratitude when you first awake, before you drift off to sleep or at any time during the day when the mood strikes. Expressing gratitude is a lovely, gentle healing practice that helps you to cultivate the mind of abundance.

1 Close your eyes, and take a few deep breaths to centre. Focus on the full extent of your wealth including the everything you own, your family and relationships, the experiences you have enjoyed, your health, your work skills and your spiritual understanding. Focus on little things such as the morning light as it streams through your window. If your mind strays to debt, or the faults in people around you, or what you feel you lack, bring your focus back to the wealth that surrounds you.

2 Visualise your reality as full of opportunity and abundance and see yourself sharing freely what you have with others. Imagine money and other forms of wealth flowing through your life. Feel confident that you will always have everything you need. When you are ready, open your eyes and end with a few more deep, relaxing breaths.

PART III

YOUR OWN MINDFULNESS BUDGET

Money has its own rules. It requires record-keeping, to keep track of the flow of your money, and a plan for spending it, called a budget. Avoiding or resisting these rules is guaranteed to create financial misery. The Mindfulness Budget, like any budget, will require you to pay attention to the rules. But unlike other budget plans, it will use the practice of mindfulness to help you align your spending to your highest values, your deepest needs and your life goals. The Mindfulness Budget will provide you with a deeply personal and highly compelling reason to follow the rules of money, and that in itself will transform your financial life.

KNOWING WHAT YOU EARN & SPEND

What is your income? What do you spend each month? If the idea of knowing precisely what you earn and spend is scary, take a deep breath and meditate for a few minutes. Relax your body and mind. If you have tightness in your neck or chest try to release it. After you have meditated for as long as you need consult your calendar and set a date for about four weeks from today for answering these questions. The process for determining your income is as follows:

1 Keep track of all your expenses for one month. Buy a small notebook and carry it with you at all times. In it you will write down *everything* you buy or spend, no matter how small or insignificant the purchase or payment. Your mortgage or rent payment, credit card payments, car payments, your bills, a packet of gum, groceries, a latte, dinner out, a haircut, a film or train fare – everything goes into your notebook. Make sure you list any direct debits made from your current account. At the end of the month you will have a fairly accurate idea of your spending patterns and where your money goes.

2 Make a separate list of any one-off or occasional expenses that you may have incurred over the past year. Some examples might be a trip to visit your family, theatre or concert tickets, car maintenance, home repairs, newspaper or magazine subscriptions, memberships or insurance payments. Using credit card statements, bank statements or actual receipts try to get an accurate idea of these expenses. When you think you have listed all these additional expenditures, add them up and divide by 12. Then add this figure to your monthly expenses under the category of 'occasional expenses'. In lieu of having a record of an entire year's spending, this will give you a more accurate picture of your average monthly outlay.

3 Develop a master list of expense categories from the items in your notebook. Try to be as accurate as possible by erring on the side of having too many categories rather than too few. For example, list groceries separately from dining out. List coffees and snacks separately from restaurant meals. You really need to see where your money is going so you can adjust your spending to fit your goals.

4 Record your spending categories on your computer using a word processing or spreadsheet programme, or software designed expressly for keeping track of income and expenses. If you are computer savvy there are many software programmes on the market to choose from. If you would rather work with paper and pencil, visit an office supply shop and buy a pad of paper or ledger book preprinted with columns and rows for entering your financial data. Work in pencil so you can easily revise your entries or correct mistakes.

5 Have your list of expense categories available. Open your small expense notebook with your expenses for the last month, and write the appropriate category tag next to each expense. Then use a calculator to add up the expenses for each category and enter the totals into your computer spreadsheet or handwritten ledger. For example, add up all your train and bus fares and enter the total in your 'public transport' category, add up your restaurant meals and enter the total under 'dining out', and add up your gum and chocolate expenses under 'snacks'. You will now have an accurate list of your expenses for the last month according to category.

6 Determine your gross monthly income. Include income from all sources such as your salary, self-employment, interest and dividends, rental income, alimony or childcare payments, and pensions. Then subtract taxes and other deductions to arrive at your net monthly income. This is what you have to work with each month. If you are self-employed use an average of your monthly income from the last six months minus any taxes that you owe.

7 Now comes the moment of truth. Subtract your monthly expenses from your monthly *net* income. You will now know if you are spending more or spending less than you earn.

Determine Your
Net Worth

◆

Set aside specific times to work on your finances over the next few weeks. You may have to face a jumbled pile of papers and records that you have been avoiding. To know the current value of what you own you may have to do some research on eBay or other auction sites. This may seem overwhelming. But once you get going you will find the process of determining your net worth more empowering than frightening.

KNOWING WHERE YOU STAND FINANCIALLY – your income, your expenses, and now your debt and assets – is an important first step for developing your Mindfulness Budget. But your Mindfulness Budget will help you do more than manage your finances. It will help you live your life mindfully, according to your highest values, in the spirit of abundance. The process of determining your net worth is as follows:

• List all your fixed assets such as your house, other real estate, your boat and cars at their current value.

• List all of your liquid assets: cash, certificates of deposit, stocks, mutual funds, bonds and bank accounts.

• List all jewellery, art, furniture, computers and other household items at their current value if you were to sell them.

• Add together all of the above. These are your total assets.

• Now, subtract all your debts such as your mortgage, car loan, personal loans and credit card balances from your total assets. The result is your net worth.

You may be shocked to learn that you have a negative net worth – in other words that you owe more than you have. Or you may be surprised that your net worth is greater than you thought. No matter what you discover rejoice in the fact that you now know where you stand. Knowing the facts about your current financial situation is empowering, and will help you make money decisions that are based in reality rather than on avoidance, fantasies or wishful thinking. It will help you decide if the way you have been handling your money is in alignment with your values and aspirations.

A MINDFUL REVIEW OF YOUR CURRENT FINANCIAL SITUATION

◆

You now have a clear picture of where you stand financially. You know how much you make after taxes, how much you spend each month, the extent of your debt and the value of what you own. If your expenses exceed your income and your debt is overwhelming your net worth, you are overspending, under-earning or both. Remember how Odysseus, the Greek hero, set his eyes on Ithaca? Before you decide how to address any financial shortfalls you may be having, you have to set your sights on your own Ithaca, the place that symbolises your authentic self, your deepest needs and your highest values.

MINDFULLY APPROACHING your financial problems with the wisdom of your highest self will prevent you from pursuing short-sighted solutions that don't serve your life goals. For example, if you are spending more than you earn getting a second job may seem a logical answer – just make more money. But having two jobs to make ends meet may be in complete conflict with your needs and values.

Finding Solutions

If you are not making enough money to meet *basic* expenses then you have to ask yourself if you need more marketable work skills, or if for some reason you are resistant to caring for yourself. There could be economic forces beyond your

control that make it very difficult for you to make a living. Company redundancies or an economic recession may be temporarily making it hard for you to make ends meet. If so, you may need to make more drastic adjustments, to weather the storm. For example, you may need to move in with a friend or consider jobs in other cities. Or you could have deep-seated issues that require counselling and emotional support to help you meet your needs and live in accordance with your values. There is no shame in needing outside help. We are all dependent on one another and each of us, at some point in our life, has turned to others for the help we need. Counselling may be just the kick-start you need to get on the road to financial health.

Who are You?

If you make a good living but your expenses exceed your income, then you may want to examine your sense of identity as it relates to your spending. You may have a conflict between your real values and your social identity. For example, your values tell you that over-consumption and the drive to have the latest electronic gadget is not good for you or society. Yet as an educated professional you feel you *need* certain things. Because your peers have a top-of-the-range mobile phone, you feel you *should* have one as well. Or, you rent a flat that is really more than you can afford because you feel it fits your identity as an up-and-coming professional. Yet when you really

get in touch with your deepest values you know it doesn't matter in the bigger scheme of things if you have the latest mobile phone or an impressive address. Your deepest self may even want to do something different with your life.

Setting Your Sights on Ithaca

Aligning your deepest values with how you live is not an easy process. And there are no rules or formulas for how to accomplish this. But using mindfulness to access your deepest self can help you let go of false identities and live in accordance with your authentic values.

Like Odysseus, with your sights set firmly on *your* Ithaca, you can create your Mindfulness Budget as a financial blueprint for the life you aspire to live. A budget that reflects your deepest needs and values will help you move towards your one-, five-, ten- and 20-year goals. It will help you avoid the Sirens of advertising, impulsive buying and over-consumption and the mindset of scarcity that conflict with your real needs, values and aspirations.

IS YOUR WORK
SATISFYING & FULFILLING?

◆

Since you now know how much income you bring home every month
— your gross income and what you net after taxes — now is a good
time to think about your satisfaction with your work. Set aside some
time to write about your work in your Mindfulness Budget journal
— at least a few hours, but if possible set aside a day. Use this time
to explore how you really feel about the work you do on a daily
basis and the career path you have chosen. If you feel you have not
chosen a career, write about what is keeping you from knowing or
focusing on a profession you want to pursue.

I F YOUR JOB is only a way to pay the bills is this acceptable
to you, or would you rather your work was more central
to who you are? Some people choose work to pay the bills so
they can pursue things they really love but that, at least at the
moment, will not support them financially. For example, you
may have a day job so you can pursue acting, or writing, or
building your sailboat in your garage, and that works for you.
Or you may be going from job to job and paying your bills,
but feeling a bit directionless and unsatisfied.

Begin by assessing how you feel about your current work
life. Ask yourself if you enjoy your work, and if so what you
enjoy about it. Do you plan to continue in your line of work
as you go forwards in life? If you are dissatisfied with your

work what don't you like about it? How and when did you decide to do the work you do? Were you influenced by your family's expectations? Or did you simply fall into your line of work through a series of events? You may not like your work, but you may feel you have to keep your job to support your family, or because you are afraid to look for other work.

Try to get beyond all your reasons for continuing with the job you have, and let yourself imagine what you really want to do. Don't worry right now whether it is practical or feasible in the near term. Allow yourself to envisage the kind of work that excites you and that you feel would nourish your soul. What would you like to do that aligns your values and ideals? Try to visualise getting up in the morning and doing the work you want to be doing. Becoming aware of what work you really want to pursue is the first step in making it a reality.

Practising Mindfulness at Work

Whether you like your job or not it will present endless opportunities to practise mindfulness. You can be mindful of the tasks you do, and supportive of your co-workers. You can practise compassion and refrain from hurtful speech or gossip. That said, you may not like the policies or culture of the company you work for, or your boss may be just plain difficult. Should you stay and try to make the best of a bad situation? When do you go? Sometimes it is hard to know. Making the best of a difficult situation can help you grow as a person, but

an emotionally toxic workplace can poison your life. If you like your work but your job is draining more than nourishing you, you may want to consider a change. Write in your journal about your ideal work situation. Do you value a beautiful work environment, good working relationships and intellectual stimulation, or do you dream of starting your own business?

Mindfulness is one of the eight steps on the Buddha's path to enlightenment. Another of the eight steps is 'right livelihood'. The practice of right livelihood requires that your work does no harm to others or the environment and contributes to society. That is a difficult standard to achieve in today's complex world. Yet when you consider what you really want to do for a living, the Buddha's simple yet profound guideline can help you sort out what work is right for you.

HOW MUCH INCOME DO YOU NEED?

Do you make enough money to cover your expenses, pay for holidays and save for your retirement? Do you want to make more money, and if so, why? That may seem like an odd question as you may think the obvious answer is yes, of course I want to make more money! But for most jobs the sky is not the limit. If you are a nurse there is a ceiling to the salary you can earn. If you love being a nurse then your financial reality is going to be tied to what you can make as a nurse. And the same limits apply for many other professions.

There are numerous professions where you can be very aggressive and earn a substantial amount of money, while your less competitive peers may make a normal middle-class salary. The point is that your profession, whilst allowing for some variance, is going to dictate your income and that in turn will determine the amount you can spend.

If one of your goals in life is to have more money – because you are not meeting your expenses, or you would like a better house, or to travel to India, or take care of your children and elderly parents – then you will have to emotionally and psychologically open yourself to that happening. When you feel ready to receive the abundance waiting for you in the universe then apply your creative mind to manifesting the abundance you desire, a part of which can be more money flowing through your life. Imagine yourself doing what you love and reaping a larger income for your efforts. If you want to enter a different profession that has more income potential, explore the ways you might do that. Or find ways to bring more money into your life doing what you currently do. Another approach is to find better ways to use the money you currently make. For example, you can cut your spending on certain things so that you have more money to use for the things you truly value.

A basic rule of thumb is that you need enough income to feel comfortable and secure in your home, to be able to pay your bills, take care of your family and have enough left over for recreation and retirement.

HOW SERIOUS IS
YOUR DEBT PROBLEM?

◆

When you calculated your net worth you added up your total debt. Knowing that figure may have frightened you or even depressed you. But better that you face reality and develop a plan to get back on your feet financially than to ignore your debt. Facing your financial problems honestly and directly is at the core of the Mindfulness Budget, as is bringing your spending into alignment with your values.

IF YOU HAVE DEBT, especially credit card debt, there are effective approaches to mitigate your obligations and reduce the balances over time. But if your problems with debt have been so severe as to be destroying your life, you may need additional help and professional intervention. Debtors' Anonymous – an international organisation with branches in several countries including the UK – uses the following questions to determine whether you have a serious problem with compulsive debt. If you answer yes to at least eight of the following 15 questions, you may need to get some professional help to get your problem under control.

- Are your debts making your home life unhappy?
- Does the pressure of debts distract you from your daily work?
- Are your debts affecting your reputation?
- Do your debts cause you to think less of yourself?

- Have you ever given false information to obtain credit?

- Have you ever made unrealistic promises to your creditors?

- Does the pressure of your debts make you care less about the welfare of your family?

- Do you ever fear that your employer, family or friends will learn the extent of your total indebtedness?

- When faced with a difficult financial situtation does the prospect of borrowing give you an inordinate sense of relief?

- Does the pressure of debt cause you to find sleeping difficult?

- Has the pressure of your debts ever caused you to consider taking drink or drugs?

- Have you ever borrowed money without giving adequate consideration to the rate of interest you are required to pay?

- Do you usually expect a negative response when you are subject to a credit investigation?

- Have you ever developed a strict regimen for paying off your debts, only to break it under pressure?

- Do you justify your debts telling yourself that you are superior to the 'other' people, and when you get your 'break' you'll be out of debt overnight?

If you answered 'yes' to eight or more of these questions, a professional counsellor can help you address those troubled aspects of your personality that are undermining your efforts to heal your relationship with money. It takes courage to seek help but you will be happy you did.

MAKE GETTING OUT OF DEBT
YOUR FIRST PRIORITY

◆

If you have determined that you don't need professional help with compulsive debt, then the first thing you need to do in creating a Mindfulness Budget is to develop a plan to reduce and eliminate your debt. There are many approaches to handling debt. In the end though, only one thing matters — you need to have a plan, and then no matter how long it takes, you need to stick to that plan and systematically reduce, and eventually eliminate, your debt. The following are preliminary steps you can take.

F ACE THE POOR FINANCIAL DECISIONS you have made, and confront the precarious financial reality you have created. Examine the ways you have used credit to fill emotional holes and bolster self-esteem. Remember to face your past actions with compassion and a spirit of forgiveness.

Let others close to you know about your debt. It will relieve you of the growing shame and worry you may be feeling, and of the need to create lies and half-truths to hide your indebtedness. Revealing your debt will help you be accountable to yourself and others, whether they are family members, friends, banks or credit card companies. It will help you to focus your energy on reducing and eliminating your debt rather than on hiding it from yourself and others.

Honour all of your debts – whether you owe the money to a credit card company, a friend or a family member. If you start living according to your highest values and honour all of your debts equally, you will be relieved from the stress and shame of living irresponsibly. You can start at this moment to turn your financial life around.

Making a Start

If you owe money to individuals meet with them and assure them you will make good on your obligations. Negotiate a payment plan that is acceptable to both you and them. If you have significant credit card debt cut up your cards now. If necessary keep one card for an emergency but avoid carrying it in your wallet or purse: the single best way to avoid the temptation to use it is to keep it at home in a drawer. Destroying your cards will require courage and willpower, but by doing so you will remove the possibility of further financial damage. Replace your previous lack of financial discipline with the discipline of living within your means. Replace the frenetic feeling of being out of control with the more calming experience of mindfulness and empowerment.

STRATEGIES FOR ELIMINATING DEBT

◆

Debt keeps you in a mental state of bondage to the past. It robs you of your present and limits your future. The following strategies require the application of mindfulness and self-discipline, but the resulting release from the burden of debt is well worth the work.

THE FIRST STRATEGY is for eliminating your credit card debt, and the second, more demanding yet highly rewarding strategy is for building your savings simultaneously as you eliminate *all* debt. Choose one that best suits your temperament.

Snowball Strategy for Eliminating Credit Card Debt

• List all your credit cards and the amounts you owe on each. Pay as much as you can on each card each month – and always pay more than the minimum.

• Educate yourself about the terms of your credit cards – interest rates, fees, grace periods, penalties for late payments, everything. Every card is different.

• Pay the most to the highest interest-rate card. With this approach, you want to pay it off first as it is costing you the most per pound of debt per month. Pay off the remaining cards in descending order.

• If possible, transfer the balances to other cards with lower interest rates, switching cards every six months if necessary. Keep track of when the low-rate period is up. The down side of switching cards frequently is that more enquiries are made on your credit report, which lowers your credit rating.

• Once you pay off the first card apply that card's payment towards your next highest rate card. For example, if you were applying £100 per month towards your highest interest card, then when it's paid off add that £100 to the next highest card on which you've been making payments of £70 per month. Now that you are paying £170 per month on the next card, you will make significant headway on your debt. This is called 'snowballing' your payments. If your final card (in this case there are three cards) has been absorbing £50 per month from you, then once your second card is paid off you will be paying £220 towards eradicating the last. At this point the credit card industry term for you is 'deadbeat' as you are no longer using their card or paying them anything.

• Once all debts are paid off begin saving the money you were paying to the credit card companies. Make clear plans to save the money, or it will more than likely disappear into your everyday expenses. Before you know it you will be buying things you don't need. So put that money where it can grow every month.

Emergency Fund Method for Eliminating *All* Debt

• List all your credit cards and the amounts you owe on each. Pay as much as you can on each card each month – and always pay more than the minimum. Make minimum payments on all your bills. Be extremely frugal, or even take on a second job, until you have saved £1,000 cash. This is your emergency fund. According to Dave Ramsey, financial guru and originator of this approach, you will never make headway in your quest to get out of debt without having something to fall back on in case you need it.

• If you already have more than £1,000 saved withdraw everything except the £1,000 and apply it to your debt. Protect the £1,000 emergency fund at all costs and do not spend it.

• List all your credit cards and the amounts you owe on each. Pay as much as you can on each card each month – and always pay more than the minimum. Create a spreadsheet of all your debts, except your mortgage. Arrange them in order of balance, from the smallest to the largest. Do everything you can to pay off the smallest debt at the top of the list whilst making minimum payments on everything else. The reason you pay off the smallest balance first is psychological – so that you have a sense of accomplishment early on, encouraging you to continue paying down your debt. If you pay off a nagging

£135 mobile phone bill, or pay a friend the £50 you have owed for a year, the psychological boost and sense of achievement carries you along to the next bill. If you have avoided paying these smaller bills, you will bring yourself into alignment with the higher value of behaving responsibly towards others.

• If for some reason a genuine emergency arises such as a car repair, and you have to spend your £1,000 emergency fund, go back to step one, refund your emergency fund and start again reducing your debts.

• After you have paid off all your debts continue to live frugally and add to your £1,000 emergency fund until you have three to six months' worth of monthly expenses put away. This will help you ease the stress and anxiety of day-to-day living, and the fear of an emergency putting you and your family in financial danger. With a three- to six-month cushion, you will have some protection from the uncertainties of life. You must keep this fund for emergencies only.

• Now that you have paid off all other debts, and put away a three- to six-month emergency fund, focus on paying off your mortgage early. Since you no longer have credit card payments, try making mortgage payments every two or three weeks instead of once per month. Apply any extra money you can find to paying off the final balance.

A MINDFUL APPRAISAL
OF YOUR POSSESSIONS

◆

When you determined your net worth you inventoried everything you owned according to its current market value. If you are in debt consider selling any items you no longer use or need to help reduce what you owe. That is the practical reason for selling such items — but there is another, equally important reason. A home filled with old, unused items, books and clothing creates stagnant energy — a kind of dead air in your home — that prevents new money and opportunities entering your life. Moving out the clutter clears out that stagnant energy — the energetic equivalent of opening the windows and letting in fresh air.

As you unearth old things in your home, you may need to be prepared to deal with the emotions that arise, because objects can trigger old memories. This is one reason we cling to our possessions. If you have trouble letting go, take a moment to meditate on impermanence, the truth that everything changes and nothing stays the same. Recall the benefit of living mindfully in the present moment rather than in the future or the past. Memories are wonderful, but ultimately they reside in our hearts, not in possessions. If you sell your great aunt's old silver set that you have *never* used and probably never *will* use you are not disrespecting her memory. You will continue to have loving memories of her without the prompting of the silver set for the rest of your life. And being from an older generation that valued thrift, she would most likely approve of you using the proceeds of the sale for reducing your debt.

• Make a master list of everything you own. Then decide what you haven't used or worn in a year. Set aside those things that may have resale value, and give away or discard the rest. Research the value of the saleable items online, and list them on a free classified website such as Craigslist; a fee-based auction site such as eBay or place an ad in the classifieds of your local newspaper. You can also consider a car-boot sale for getting rid of less expensive items that would be too tedious to sell online. If you have books you haven't looked at in years gathering dust on your bookshelf, consider selling them on Amazon or donate them to your local library.

• Take the proceeds of everything you sell and apply it to your credit card debt. If you are debt-free deposit your earnings in a savings account.

Negative Spending Patterns

After a month of keeping track of your expenses you know how you have been spending your money. Although you may be surprised, it will be clear to you now where your money is going. Assess each expense category and decide if:

• You are spending too much in that category in relation to your income.

• You are buying things that you do not need, or things that do not align with your authentic self, your deepest needs, or the values you would like to live by.

If you are spending in ways that are putting you into debt or undermining the life you really want, then you need to make adjustments in how you spend your money. And after you make those changes try to identify the habits and emotional triggers that may have led you to spend in ways that are harming you.

Why did You Buy those Shoes?

If, for example, you spent a shocking amount on shoes during the month, try to remember how you were feeling when you bought them. See if any patterns emerge. With reflection you may realise that you buy expensive shoes when you are feeling insecure. You can lower the amount you allow for shoes in your budget, but if you do not have a strategy to overcome the emotional triggers or societal pressures that caused you to overspend in the first place you will continue to overspend. This is the essence of the Mindfulness Budget – becoming fully conscious and aware of the reasons for which you spend, save, borrow or give, and making sure you do so in ways that support the life you really want.

The Myth of Sisyphus

The practice of mindfulness helps you to address habitual, negative thinking, feeling and behaviour patterns that sabotage your success, happiness and well-being. These patterns are so ingrained that you may think you have no power to change them. You may feel like Sisyphus, the character in the Greek myth, condemned by the god Zeus for his bad deeds to roll a rock up a hill, only to have it roll right back down before he could get it to the top. He had to repeat this task daily for eternity. Everyday, like Sisyphus, you hope you can curb your overspending and roll that rock up the hill, but out of habit you impulsively buy that latte, or that great dress you saw on sale, and down the rock comes.

Breaking the Spell

Sisyphus was under a spell, a severe punishment from the gods, and you may feel the same. You have tried to get control of your finances, but, like Sisyphus, every night you find yourself at the bottom of the hill, deeper in debt than you were yesterday. You feel confused, overwhelmed and defeated. So how do you break the spell or curse that keeps you nslaved to your negative relationship with money?

First of all, Sisyphus bought into the absurdity of the sentence, and kept rolling that ball up the hill and back down. If he lived today he might have felt condemned (by the twin gods of marketing and advertising) to forever consume things

to feel good about himself, to compete with others for status and power, to live in fear of losing everything he has, to go into debt buying things he can't afford to appear more successful than he is, and to work at a job he doesn't like.

Freedom of Choice

Like Sisyphus we perpetuate our own suffering, by buying into the false promises of materialism and consumerism. We create our own interminable sentences by living lives that are stressful and unfulfilling. But we don't have to live that way. Imagine if Sisyphus would have said to Zeus, 'This is a myth! I don't have to push that rock up and down ever again if I don't want to. I don't have to buy a new car this year, I don't need a bigger house than my sister and brother-in-law and I don't have to buy something when I'm feeling insecure or down. I don't have to pretend things will magically be different tomorrow even though I continue to do the same things that have landed me in financial trouble today. And, I don't have to suffer because I am free to choose to think, feel and do things differently.'

Put Down the Rock

You can put down the rock of your critical voice, and those of others, that are draining your life force. You can let go of your fear of doing those things that will uplift you and align with your true needs. If you feel insecure you don't have to turn to spending to ease your pain. You can challenge the myth that

buying something will make you feel better. You can walk away from the gods of consumerism and instead meditate on loving kindness towards yourself and unconditional self-acceptance. Addressing your insecurity directly releases you from the bondage of negative spending. Spending habits that are causing you harm can feel as powerful as addictions. Invoking your higher wisdom, and challenging the myths that keep you addicted, is the way to lessen their hold on you.

A MINDFUL STRATEGY FOR
OVERCOMING ADDICTION TO SPENDING

In the morning when you first wake up, spend a few minutes being mindful of your breath. Breathe into your abdomen and relax your body as much as possible. Feel your body as you slowly breathe in and out. Let your breath generate a sense of spaciousness in your mind and body. Try to memorise this feeling, and use it as your reference point to come back to for the rest of the day.

As you go about your day you may notice your breathing tends to get tighter and you become less aware of your connection to your body. You may find you are more and more caught up in your worries and thoughts. When this happens you will find that you are more vulnerable to negative habitual behaviours such as compulsive buying or overspending.

Remember to Breathe

Your breath is an exquisite biofeedback system. It will show you when you are losing connection with yourself – your true needs, values and goals. If you begin to train yourself to feel whenever your body and breathing are contracted, and when you are taking shallow breaths or not breathing at all, you can intervene in that impulse to spend unwisely. When you feel you 'have to have' something, or you feel pulled by advertising to buy something, stop and notice that you are feeling this

way. Then soften and relax your body and begin to take deep, slow breaths. The deep, slow breaths will bring you out of your head and into your body and into the sense of peace and spaciousness you felt in your morning meditation.

Satisfying Your Hunger

As you allow your body to relax and your breathing to open you may feel the hunger you had for the thing you wanted to buy dissipating, and in its place a deeper hunger being satisfied. This is the hunger to be deeply connected to your authentic self and your authentic needs. So, when the hunger of compulsion appears, rather than heading to the shops take a moment to relax and breathe. If there is something deeper to explore, a feeling of anger or depression or insecurity driving you to overspend, then through the breath you will begin know what that is. Then you can empower yourself by directly dealing with what is troubling you.

A Mindful Analysis of
Three Spending Categories

Everyone spends money in ways that are unique to each individual. But there are certain expense categories that almost everyone has. Take some time to reflect mindfully on the three expense areas that we tend to have in common — housing, food and local transport. When you create your Mindfulness Budget, try to bring this in-depth analysis to your other categories of spending.

Housing & Home Furnishings

Whether you rent or own your home, your housing expense is often one of the largest items in your budget, so getting this expenditure right in all ways — emotionally, spiritually and financially — is a good place to start in building your Mindfulness Budget. Ideally, your living space is comfortable, safe and adequate for your needs — whether you live alone or with others. But if you are unhappy with the physical space in which you live then the following questions may provide some clarity:

• Are you living in the city, town, village or area where you want to be living?

• Is your flat or house the right size? The real issue is whether it is adequate for you. If your living space is too small and uncomfortable it may cause you emotional distress — but if too large it may feel more burdensome than comfortable.

• Is your building block or home well maintained, clean and free of insects or pests? If you own your home are you overwhelmed with garden and lawn care, home repairs and renovation projects?

• If you rent do you have a fair and responsible landlord who takes care of repairs promptly? If your building has difficult, irresponsible management it may be causing you continual low-level stress.

• Do you feel safe and secure in your neighbourhood? On-going worry about your physical safety can take a toll on your mental health.

• Are you close to public transport if you need it?

• Is your home or flat close enough to your family and friends to allow you to socialise often?

• Do you like your neighbours? If you have difficult relationships with your neighbours the lack of peace and goodwill will wear on you.

• Do you hear the neighbours or street noise? Noise pollution can feel invasive and stressful.

• If you have a car do you struggle to find parking?

These are all quality-of-life issues, and you may think they have nothing to do with creating a budget. But a Mindfulness Budget takes into consideration how you think and feel about every area of your life. How you feel about where you live is as important as how much you pay for your mortgage or rent.

No flat or house is perfect, but if your current living situation has more negatives than positives, you may want to consider looking for a new flat or home that provides a more comfortable and healing environment in which to live. On a spiritual level you need more than a house. You need a home for both body and soul.

How Much do You Pay?

After you've considered these quality-of-life issues take a look at how much you are paying. Your housing cost needs to be in balance with your income or you will feel the pressure and stress of being rent- or mortgage- poor. And if too much money is going towards housing it makes it difficult for you to have what you need in other areas of your life.

How much do you pay for your rent or mortgage? A good rule of thumb is between 28 per cent and 35 per cent of your monthly gross income. Of course, it depends on the market where you live, with some cities being more expensive than others. If you are paying a mortgage your monthly cost should be no more than 1 per cent of your purchase. That would include mortgage payment, insurance, taxes and upkeep. So if you buy a £250k home, your payments should be around £2,500 per month on a 30-year fixed loan.

If you are paying too much for your mortgage or rent first examine why you are doing so. Do you want the status of an affluent neighbourhood even though you really can't afford it?

Are you struggling to pay your rent or mortgage because you lost your job? Or do you live in a modest flat or home but are failing to make enough to meet basic expenses? If you answered yes to any of these questions you may need to consider a different living situation; one that is in balance with your income and provides the best quality of life possible. You may need to downsize, share or live with relatives until you can increase your income. Or you may be living in a very expensive city and need to consider a more affordable location to live and work.

Be realistic about what you can afford right now, and forgive yourself if you have been spending more than you should. Your long-term goals may include moving to a larger, more comfortable flat, or buying a bigger house in a more desirable location. With a realistic assessment of your current income and expenses and by living within your means, you can reach your goals in the future by living mindfully and responsibly in the present.

Creature Comforts

Home furnishings – sofas, chairs, beds, dining tables, window coverings, rugs and kitchen appliances – can take up a large portion of your budget, or not… So much depends on your needs, your motivation to spend and your income. Reflect on the following questions before deciding on how much to allow for home furnishings in your budget.

Is your home environment comfortable, welcoming and aesthetically pleasing to you? Or are you living with a shabby sofa or depressing wall colours because you feel you can't afford to buy new furniture or hire a painter? You may want to shift your thinking and consider thrift shops and online sites where you can find well-made furniture in good condition at a fraction of its original price. Then add a weekend painting party with friends, provide the pizza and beer, and transform your drab flat or house into a warm, cosy, comforting place that you can call home.

Second-hand

Almost everything for your home can be found second-hand. In affluent cultures many high value items are discarded to make room for the latest versions. If you have champagne tastes and a beer income, by shopping second-hand you can most certainly find great items that will provide the champagne décor you want but at a beer price. It's possible to have the beautiful home you want right now for very little money. If you feel you *should* be able to afford new items ask yourself where this 'should' is coming from? Are you embarrassed by the idea of shopping at a second-hand shop? These are good questions that circle back to knowing your true needs, values and goals. If your true need is to have a beautiful, comfortable home try not to let fears about what others think prevent you having what you really need and want.

Are You Buying Now, Paying Later?

On the other hand, do you spend too much on new furniture, rugs, kitchen gadgets and appliances, sheets, towels, curtains and other decor? If you do, is your spending on home furnishings in line with your income, or is a lot of it going on your credit card? Furniture shops often offer expensive items such as beds, sofas and dining tables on a 'buy now, pay later' basis. And it is easy to get in over your head buying expensive furniture on credit. In addition TV shopping channels offer 'deals' on home furnishings 24 hours a day. In either case the advertised 'deal' is often more than many can really afford. If you are overspending, practise expressing gratitude for the beautiful home you already have.

Who are You Trying to Impress?

If you are trying to impress others with expensive home furnishings and decor and other material possessions, ask yourself if that motivation is in line with your highest values. If you are still overly worried about what others think, or you feel insecure about your self-worth, take time to meditate on self-love and compassion. You are fine just as you are. Furnish and decorate your home in a style that pleases you and the people you live with. Spend a realistic amount that is in balance with your income, and try not to worry what others think. If you feel good in your home and enjoy your surroundings that is all that matters.

Groceries & Dining Out

Because you kept track of your expenses for a month, you have a good idea of the combined amount that you spend on groceries and dining in restaurants. You also know what you spend on snacks and coffees. If you stop for coffee in the morning, eat out daily for lunch or bring home takeaways for dinner several times a week, and then eat dinner at restaurants over the weekend, your total food bill is one area to examine closely if you want to save money.

First assess how much you are spending on coffee and snacks. If the monthly amount is higher than you realised, consider not doing that for a month. Buy good coffee and take it to work in a flask. Then bring your snacks to work rather than buy them.

To reduce your overall food budget learn to cook or become a better cook. If you cook more, you will eat out less. Your grocery bill may be somewhat higher, but if you stop eating out as much as you are, your overall food bill will plummet. A mindfully prepared home-cooked meal can be nourishing for both body and soul.

Do you buy 'junk food'? Junk foods are over-processed packed foods, loaded with fats, salt, sugar and preservatives of dubious nutritional value. Try to bring home more organic fruits and vegetables, wholegrains and pulses. Buy organic dairy and chicken and wild-caught fish. Eat less beef and when you do make sure it was grass fed. You will be healthier and more mindful of what you are putting into your body.

Too tired after work to cook? Spend some time at the weekend preparing a few dishes ahead of time that you can warm up when you get home. Add a salad and a glass of wine and you will quickly have a relaxing home-cooked meal. Search the web or borrow cookery books from your local library to find recipes for quick, satisfying meals.

If you are struggling to get out of debt or make ends meet consider the benefits of taking a packed lunch to work. You will have more control over the quality of what you eat and you can bring delicious leftovers from the great dinner you cooked the night before. Buying lunch seems inexpensive day-to-day but they can put quite a dent in your budget.

After you have considered these ideas decide on an amount for groceries and an amount for eating out that makes sense for you, and save it to enter in your Mindfulness Budget.

If you are tempted to eat fast food or buy junk food, practise the 'body mindfulness' exercise on pages 46–47.

Avoid Food Wastage

Whether you buy groceries and eat at home or buy your meals from restaurants, food is an essential purchase. Keeping a close eye on your overall food bill can help you save significant amounts of money. Even if you mostly eat at home the common problem of food wastage – letting food spoil before you eat it – can ruin your food budget. In a disorganised fridge leftovers can get buried behind other items and go off.

Plan Ahead

Overbuying can also wreak havoc on your food budget. If you go to the supermarket with a vague idea of what you are going to need in the next few days, you set yourself up for buying more than you can eat. Then you risk losing it to spoilage. You can avoid this by planning your meals. It sounds like yet another thing to do in your busy schedule, but the time you spend will pay off in savings at the till.

Try planning for three days – breakfast, lunch and dinner plus snacks – and see how you do. Check your refrigerator and store cupboards to evaluate what you have to hand. Build your meal ideas around what you need to use up, and then develop a grocery list of items to complete your three-day menu. Try to consume all the food you bought. If you have leftovers try freezing them.

Local Transport

Unless you work at home or live close enough to walk, you need transport to get to work. This is most likely a car, a bus or a train, but it could be a motorcycle or a bicycle. A car can be one of the most expensive items you will purchase other than your home. Car payments, car insurance, petrol, parking, vehicle excise duty, and maintenance and repairs can quickly eat a big hole in your budget. A new car starts losing its value from the moment you drive it off the forecourt. It pays to reflect on why you have a car and if you really need one.

Questions About Owning a Car:

• Do you really need a car or can you manage with walking or public transport?

• Is having a car part of your identity? Would you feel insecure if you didn't have one? Is the make and model of the car important to your identity? For example, would you be embarrassed to be seen in a budget model compact car? Do you feel you need to have a newer, more expensive car to impress others?

• Go back to your record of expenses for a month and review the amount you spent on your car. Include the total of car payments, petrol, maintenance, vehicle excise duty, parking and insurance for the month. Are you surprised at how much owning a car costs or did you already know?

• What is the yearly cost of owning your car?

• What did you pay for it and what is it worth today? How much has the value of your car depreciated?

Questions About Public Transport:

• If you take public transport to work do you find it enjoyable or stressful?

• Is public transport convenient to where you live?

• Do you feel safe taking public transport?

• Are you able to go without owning a car because you make use of public transport?

• Do you wish you owned a car?

Alternatives to Owning a Car

Have you considered a bicycle or motor scooter as a way to get around your neighbourhood or to commute to work? Cities are becoming more bicycle friendly, providing dedicated bike lanes and facilities to park and lock up your bicycle. For short commutes, and if the route is safe, a bicycle might save you significant amounts of money. Even if you own a car for longer trips, cycling is a good option for your health and budget.

Car hire companies in larger cities in the UK are experimenting with a pay-as-you-go alternative to owning your own car. These cars can be booked by the hour, day or as long as you want – short enough to do your weekly shopping or long enough for getting away on a weekend. The companies take care of insurance, vehicle excise duty, maintenance and cleaning. The cars are booked online 24 hours a day, seven days a week or by phone. You unlock the car with your membership card, enter your PIN number and drive away. When you return the car at the end of your booking, you lock it with your membership card and walk away. The best thing is that you only pay for a car when you need one, which can save you thousands of pounds a year.

REVIEWING YOUR VALUES, NEEDS & GOALS

The final step before you construct your Mindfulness Budget is to write a paragraph that concisely expresses your highest values, your deepest needs and your personal life goals. This is at the very heart of your Mindfulness Budget, and what distinguishes the Mindfulness Budget from other financial self-help programmes. It ensures that your motivation for getting your financial life in order comes from within you. To help you on your journey to financial health you will be asked to refer to your statement on a daily basis.

YOUR HIGHEST VALUES are the qualities, standards or principles that you use to guide your actions. If you notice a particular person is consistently courageous or generous you can be sure that quality reflects his or her deepest priorities in life. A brave person speaks out, even when it's dangerous to do so. A generous person selflessly gives money or time to help others. Besides courage and generosity other common values are acceptance, beauty, commitment, excellence, honesty, family, joy, harmony, health, leadership, love, compassion, respect, service, spirituality and abundance.

Living according to your highest values will make it easier for you to make sound financial decisions, and intervene when external forces and emotional vulnerabilities tempt you to overspend. For example, if you value your health, you will stop buying junk food, if you value commitment you will work to stick to your budget, or if you value love you will have the courage to love and be loved rather than attempting to make do with material possessions. If you value honesty you will honestly assess whether what you want to buy is a wise purchase.

Everyone has personal values, even if they haven't given them much thought. Some you inherited from your parents, teachers and other influential people in your life. Others were absorbed from the culture around you, the place where you live and your peers. Before you create your Mindfulness Budget take time to reflect on which values are most important to you today, at this time in your life. List your values in your Mindfulness Budget journal. Describe them in detail and give examples of how they inform your life.

Knowing your values helps you:

• **Have a clear set of guidelines for your financial life.** You're less likely to spend in ways that undermine your real needs and long-term goals.

• **Make good financial decisions.** You quickly know what are good choices for yourself and what are not.

• **Live with integrity.** Your actions are congruent with the things you hold most dear.

• **Manage stress.** The more you live true to your values the more fulfilled and peaceful you are.

Your Deepest Needs

When it comes to money many of us have a very difficult time distinguishing between our needs and wants. In prehistoric times our basic needs were simple. We needed shelter from the elements, food and water, clothing, and protection from danger. Fast-forward to today and our definition of basic needs has changed dramatically. Now we need a roof over our heads (as opposed to a cave or more primitive structure), healthy food and bottled water, a varied wardrobe, utilities (heat, electric and water), phone, and transport. Then what about cable or satellite TV, a mobile phone, Internet access and haircuts? Are these basic needs? It depends on what you feel is basic for your life. For most of us, the line between basic needs and wants is blurred. When you develop your Mindfulness Budget you will assess each spending category to determine if it is a need or a want and if you can afford what you are currently spending.

Reflect on Your Deepest Needs

But before you make that determination it is important to reflect on your deepest needs. Your basic needs are usually practical in nature. Your deepest needs are often emotional, psychological or spiritual. Knowing your deepest needs and acting on them in positive ways will help you distinguish between your basic needs and wants, and help you to allocate your financial resources more wisely.

Your deepest needs might include to love and feel loved, to feel respected and appreciated, to have the companionship of family and friends, to feel safe and secure, to express yourself artistically, to have work that is rewarding, to feel of service to others, to connect to nature, to heal your body, to recover from emotional wounding, to engage in a spiritual path, and to address the deeper mysteries of life such as what happens after you die.

Empower Yourself From Within

So much of our irrational approach to spending comes from not being in touch with our deepest needs and not finding positive, constructive and effective ways to meet those needs in our lives. For example, having an expensive house you can't afford may impress others but will not deliver the respect you are really craving. But addressing your self-esteem issues and living by your higher values might bring the *self*-respect you deeply desire, making the house and other people's opinion unnecessary. Buying things will not fill the hole in you that longs to love and be loved. Yet, out of fear of intimacy and rejection, you may continue to haunt the shops. Buying an expensive car to appear powerful and successful will not make you so. On the other hand, empowering yourself from within, through spiritual practice or psychotherapy, will make external reassurance unnecessary. When you know your deepest needs your need for external approval falls away.

A Breath of Fresh Air

Advertising agencies thrive on tapping into deep needs such as our desire for intimacy or our need to feel peace and contentment in a stressful world. An ad for an air freshener may promise fresh air, relaxation and the peaceful experience of nature. Yet the air freshener is not really providing fresh air: it is filling your room with chemicals. The chemicals may have a pleasing scent but they are still chemicals. And then the air freshener isn't inherently relaxing or natural. In reality it is a small plastic thing that you plug into your wall.

If you want to have fresh air in your home, or you want to relieve your stress and connect with nature, a better choice would be to open your windows or go for a relaxing walk. Advertising excels at providing you with ersatz solutions to meeting your deepest needs. Because we struggle to both know our deepest needs and address them, we are vulnerable to those who would use our deepest needs and desires to manipulate us.

What's Holding You Back?

Find time to be alone and undisturbed. Try to identify your deepest needs. Which ones are you working to meet and which ones are you not addressing? Write about the ways you are meeting some of your deepest needs. How successful have you been? Then write about those needs you have had trouble meeting. What might you do to begin to address them? What is holding you back?

Your Life Goals

Imagine you are living according to your highest values and you are working daily to meet your deepest needs. What would your life look like? Is it a different life than you are living today? What changes, if any, would you have to make? What would you be doing for a living? Where would you be living and with whom? Are you living in a different house or flat, or have you moved to a different city? What would a typical day in your life be like? If you have always valued nature are you living in a rural area? If not do you spend more time in nature on the weekends? Or if you love the city have you left the suburbs and now enjoy the pleasures of a more urban lifestyle? Have you returned to school to upgrade your skills or train for a new profession?

Without getting bogged down in your current situation and allowing it to limit your ability to visualise the future, think about the life you would like to be living. This is not an exercise in fantasy, but rather a creative visualisation of what you would like to manifest in your life.

A Year From Now...

Where would you like to be and what would you like to be doing a year from now? Write about the life you want in your journal. Add photos or drawings to inspire you. As you write, note any negativity that may be coming from the family voices in your head, or from your friends and peers. For example,

you may have feelings of doubt arise if you want to downsize and live in a smaller house, or live in a way that your upwardly mobile friends may find perplexing and unappealing. Or if you want to make more money as a professional doing what you love, you may fear that your family members and friends who struggle financially may feel threatened. If these negative voices intrude, have a mental conversation with the people attached to the voices. Let them know you love them *and* you also need to live in alignment with your values and who you really are. Imagine them smiling at you and supporting you.

Making it Happen

If you have mentally been living day-to-day and financially pay cheque to pay cheque, this process of imagining and visualising the life you want may seem both exciting and daunting. You may have been avoiding thinking about the future because you fear you are not capable of creating the life you want. When those fears arise take a few deep breaths and let the fear wash over you. It is OK to get in touch with your highest values and your deepest needs and imagine the life you really want. When you have created a vision of what you want your life to be, it is time to move on to the practicalities of making it happen. Making changes will change your relationships, but do not let that deter you either. If your partner truly loves you he or she will support you and want you to be happy. There is no better time to start than now.

List Your Goals

Write down your goals for the next year, and then for the next five, ten and 20 years. Focusing on your goals for the next year, generate specific tasks for each goal and attach a time estimate next to each task. For example, if you want to move to a less expensive flat within six months, then one task may be to investigate the neighbourhoods where you might live. Decide on a time frame for completing that task. Assigning tasks to goals is an important step. Otherwise, without specific tasks assigned to them, goals will remain ideas and aspirations and will never manifest in reality.

The paradox of generating goals for your future is that in the process of working towards them, you begin to manifest the life you want in the present moment. For example, you may have a goal to live in a rural area. Although you still live in a city, you can begin this weekend to spend more time in the area where you want to live; and if your goal is to be debt free in the future you can begin immediately to take charge of your finances so that your spending serves your deepest needs and highest values.

Your Values, Needs & Goals Statement

Write a paragraph in your journal that summarises your highest values, your deepest needs and your life goals. The process of condensing a lot of thought and feeling into the space of a paragraph will help you clarify how you really want to live

your life. In turn, this process will give you a strong foundation for creating your Mindfulness Budget and provide you with a set of principles to guide you in how you spend your money going forwards. These are not external principles dictated by an outside authority: these are your principles based on your highest values, deepest needs and personal life goals. Place your statement where you can see it on a daily basis and keep a copy in your purse or wallet.

CREATE YOUR
MINDFULNESS BUDGET

◆

Creating your Mindfulness Budget is somewhat like putting togeth-er a puzzle. Each part of the puzzle is dependent on the other to make the whole. This is why mindfulness is so important in creating a budget. You have to do the hard work of closely examining all the pieces of the puzzle before you can construct a budget that serves you well. Your Mindfulness Budget will reflect who you are.

A MINDFULNESS BUDGET requires becoming mindful of what you think and feel about everything that impacts your financial life – your work, your income, your expenses, what you own, your debt, your net worth, your obligations to your family and so on. If you have been avoiding looking at these issues the process so far may have been challenging. If your spending habits are dysfunctional and your financial decisions have been irresponsible, this has no doubt been a difficult journey. Finally, the Mindfulness Budget requires you to get in touch with your deepest needs and highest values, and to know your personal life goals – a challenge for any of us, but hopefully a most uplifting and rewarding one.

In the previous sections you have been invited to do this soul-searching work, and to record your discoveries and real-isations in your Mindfulness Budget journal. Congratulations if you have come this far! Of course, the work is ongoing, and new realisations are waiting in your future. But at this point you can begin to construct a Mindfulness Budget using as a basis your monthly income and expense sheet and your net worth statement from your journal (see pages 91–92).

Let's Get Started

To create your Mindfulness Budget start by reading your statement of values, needs and goals and place it where you can see it. Then refer to the monthly income and expense record you have already created (see pages 88–90).

Review each expense category and amount and decide if it is in alignment with your needs, values and goals statement. Mark those expense categories where you may be overspending in relation to your income. For example, you may be able to see now that you are spending too much on groceries or eating out, or on clothes, computer games or cosmetics. Review each expenses category and decide if it is a 'need' or a 'want'. In other words is it a basic need or is it something you could live without? If you are in serious debt or have just lost your job, begin paring away at the 'wants' until you get on your feet.

You may decide to eliminate some categories altogether if they do not align with your values, needs and goals statement. For example, you may decide to eliminate buying and playing computer games because they take too much time away from working towards your goals. Or you may want to add a new expense category. For example, if through reflection on your deepest needs you realise you want to develop your artistic talents, you may decide to eliminate magazine subscriptions and shift the money from that category to buying art supplies.

After you have assessed your categories and expenses from the perspective of your authentic needs, values and goals, if you have not yet listed them add spending categories for debt reduction, savings and giving. Even if it is a small amount you must save something each month. If possible practise giving by donating to charity each month.

Now review each expense category you have decided to keep and make adjustments to bring your total expenses in line with your current income.

How to Work With Your Mindfulness Budget

Review your statement of values, needs and goals on a daily basis. Having a clear sense of what matters most to you will help you stay on track, and make you less vulnerable to impulse buying and the pull of advertising. The following activities will help you stay focused:

• Practise breath or mindfulness meditation on a daily basis (see pages 36–37 and 42–43). Meditate on your breath to relax, and practise mindfulness meditation to help you stay in touch with your body, your emotions and your thought patterns. Practising mindfulness meditation keeps you in touch with your authentic self.

• If you are not working with a computer programme, print out copies of your budget. Use one for each month. Make sure you have space for entering your actual expense amounts next to each budget category. If you are using a ledger book, dedicate a page or more for each month, whatever you need.

• Commit to reducing and eliminating all debt.

• Cut up your credit cards, keeping one for emergencies.

• Continue to keep track of everything you spend using whatever method works for you.

• At the end of every month, make sure you total your expenses for each category and enter the actual amounts next to your budgeted amounts.

• Review each category and determine whether you have overspent or under-spent.

• If you have bought things outside of your budget categories, create a miscellaneous category, but make a note of each item you bought. Note if these extra items caused you to overspend for the month, or if you already made spending adjustments to allow for them.

• Determine if you have overspent or under-spent in your total expenses for the month. If you overspent, reflect on why you did and in what categories you overspent. Recommit to staying on track.

• If you need to adjust your budgeted amounts to reflect changes in your income or expenses, do it at the end of the month. An example would be a change in your housing cost because you took on a room-mate.

• Balance your current account every month.

• Review your credit card statements monthly to make sure they are accurate and your payments have been recorded.

• Go through your receipts at the end of the month and keep those you need for warranty or tax purposes.

• Keep financial records organised in a safe place. For example, your lease, mortgage, bank statements and tax records.

• Every three months review how you have been doing financially. Have you been consistently reducing your debt, staying on budget and working towards meeting your authentic needs and goals? If you have been consistently overspending in some areas write in your journal about the emotional or psychologi-

cal reasons behind your overspending. Create positive strategies to intervene in your tendency to overspend. And be loving and compassionate towards yourself.

• If your financial situation changes dramatically create a new Mindfulness Budget that reflects your current financial situation. For example if you lost your job, you may need to cut spending drastically in some areas. If you got married you may want to ask your spouse to create a Mindfulness Budget with you for your shared expenses. If you received a substantial raise you may want to rethink your Mindfulness Budget, but make sure you base your new budget on your Values, Needs and Goals Statement.

• Review your values, needs and goals statement yearly and revise it if necessary.

INDEX

FURTHER READING

Money

Joe Dominguez and Vicki Robin. *Your Money or Your Life: 9 Steps to Transforming Your Relationship with Money and Achieving Financial Independence: Revised and Updated for the 21st Century*. New York: Penguin, 2008.

J. D. Roth. *Your Money: The Missing Manual*. Sebastopol, CA: O'Reilly Media, Inc., 2010

Suze Orman. *Women and Money: Owning the Power to Control Your Destiny*. New York: Random House, 2010

Ken Clark. *The Complete Idiot's Guide To Getting Out of Debt*. New York: Penguin, 2009.

Lynne Twist. *The Soul of Money: Reclaiming the Wealth of Our Inner Resources*. New York: W. W. Norton & Company, 2006.

George Kinder. *The Seven Stages of Money: Understanding the Spirit and Value of Money in Your Life*. New York: Dell, 2000.

Mindful Budgeting

Kulananda and Dominic Houlder. *Mindfulness and Money: The Buddhist Path of Abundance*. New York: Broadway, 2003.

Allan Hunt Badiner, ed. *Mindfulness in the Marketplace: Compassionate Responses to Consumerism*. Berkeley, CA: Parallax Press, 2002.

Richard Payne. *How Much Is Enough? Buddhism, Consumerism, and the Human Environment*. Sommerville, MA: Wisdom Publications, 2010.

Deborah Knuckey. *Conscious Spending for Couples: Seven Skills for Financial Harmony*. Hoboken, NJ: John Wiley & Sons, Inc., 2003.

Mindfulness

Thich Nhat Hanh. *Peace is Every Step: The Path of Mindfulness in Everyday Life*. New York: Bantam, 1991.

Bante Henepola Gunaratana. *Mindfulness in Plain English*. Sommerville, MA: Wisdom Publications, 2002.

Jon Kabat-Zinn. *Coming to Our Senses: Healing Ourselves and the World Through Mindfulness*. New York: Hyperion, 2006